Ann –

Cinderella will always be home!

When Normal Blew Up

The Story of the People Who Died and the People Who Lived On

If you like **When Normal Blew Up**
please write a review
on Amazon.com and Goodreads.com.
Thank you.

 **Red Raku Press**
ENJOYMENT COMFORT CHEER
www.redrakupress.com

Photographs used with permission courtesy of:
    The Historical & Genealogical Library of Pickaway County
    Karen Schieber Donnelly
    Jim Willison
    Arnold Holbrook
    Teresa Grant Gilmore

Circleville emblem used with permission courtesy of Janet Wittich

Photo on front cover used with permission courtesy of Circleville City Schools.

Cover design by Lynn Starner Design

For information contact:

Red Raku Press
www.redrakupress.com

ISBN-10: 0-9987203-0-5
ISBN-13: 978-0-9987203-0-2

Everyone thinks that awful comes by itself, but it doesn't. It comes hand in hand with normal. - Brian Doyle[1]

In Memory

I have never considered it too important the mortality of man. The promise of entering into the Kingdom of Heaven or subject to the fiery depths of Hell are somewhat meaningless to me. The mortality for which I strive is in the hearts of men. For on my demise other men should say, he led a good life, or other men should remember some small contribution that I have (or might have) made for the good of mankind...

...To me the mark of manhood is the ability to master adversity. The road of life is not always an easy one. Nor do I see any reason that it should be.

-- Ted Foster (excerpt from an undated journal entry written in longhand, found by my mom in my dad's desk after his death.)

Saturday, April 15, 1967

A man walked into an old-fashioned drug store on a busy Saturday and laid a smoking package on the pharmacy counter in the back. He shouted for everyone to leave -- he had a bomb. The store owner grabbed the package and ran down the back hallway. The man chased the owner, grabbed him, and struggled to take the package away. A pharmacist saw what was happening, raced after both, and tried to pull the two apart. A clerk was standing at the back door. A bookkeeper was in the back office, unaware. The bomb went off. (*The entirety of the story I knew growing up.*)

Those Who Died

Charles Schieber, 48, proprietor and pharmacist, survived by his wife, Jean, and two children: Larry and Karen.

Ted Foster, 38, pharmacist, survived by his wife, Eileen, and five children: Karen, Ty, Joni, Robert, and Donald.

Martha "Mart" Lagore, 45, clerk, survived by her husband, Lawrence (Lonnie), and two children: Linda and Gary.

Francis "Pam" Willison, 36, bookkeeper, survived by her husband, Charles (Chuck) and three children: Richard, Jim and Gary.

Lee Holbrook (bomber), 40, laborer at Eshelman's Feed Mill, survived by his wife, Phyllis and three children.

Table of Contents

INTRODUCTION

Nine

I was nine when it happened. Where did time go? Fifty years later and I am still haunted by this event, the illogical tragedy that occurred in the little town of Circleville, Ohio, in 1967: the bombing of Bingman's Drug Store by a jealous husband. My dad, Ted Foster, a pharmacist at the store, left behind a grieving wife and five young children.

My family rarely talked about the event, and when we did, we only talked in whispers and sketches. I asked every twenty years or so for a remembrance, but my family was at a loss for words. What was there to say? It happened; we were sad; we moved on. That was the sum total of our processing of the event. I took my cues from them and understood it was taboo to talk about that day or the dead.

Last summer, my mom passed away. She was eulogized at the Community United Methodist Church by a young preacher nine "preacher-generations" removed from the knowledge of the tragedy that befell Circleville. As we sat around a conference table at the church preparing the preacher for the service, we were surprisingly compelled to tell him about our family and our relationship to the church as defined by that moment almost five decades before. We talked about the event, the double funeral at this very church, how afterward the church raised us and kept us, as in the Bible verse.[2]

It seemed like very old history. My brothers and sister and I had moved away years ago; my aging mom and stepdad in the past decade had been unable to attend services regularly or be active in the affairs of the church as in the past. But my family nonetheless still felt an ownership of this church; and the church owned our hearts, tethered by an invisible connection to the worst day of our lives. The flood of memories rekindled my desire to know more, so I embarked on a mission: to audaciously break the taboo and talk to people outside of my family about what happened.

By the time that I found the nerve, though, most of the victim's spouses and many of the first responders had already gone on to their glory. All who remained, those who might remember, were of the advanced age where recall fades and details become sketchy. Yet, with the help of family and friends, I started a conversation.

Remarkably, many people were ready to share their story. Stories that, many told me, they had never shared with anyone before. Stories that were held sacred. It was as if, for all these years, we had protected our collective memories from the light, precious bundles held tightly, silently, and dearly to our hearts. We had held our memories so close to the chest, without sharing, that we could still feel the intensity of the emotions they packed, and the blast of grief threatened to overwhelm us. Paradoxically, in the telling and retelling of our stories, we were finally able to find some distance from the pain, and our memories lost some of their staggering impact.

Still, we never wanted to lose those feelings completely, because they were all that kept us connected to the people we had lost. If we let go too much, would the memories of our loved ones fade? Eventually disappear? That's why I needed to write this story, so I wouldn't forget.

The tale is, after all, at its core, one of horror and sorrow. I worried about how to hold the conversations and write the story in a way that wouldn't re-traumatize people. I longed for a story that could be healing, not just for me but for those I interviewed and others who might read it. I was driven to lay out what happened in excruciating detail, to finally hold in my memory a complete and full picture of the event, not just the two or three sentences that I knew growing up. I also wanted to find the truth and dispel the rumors and false details that had floated about all these years.

I quickly became aware that telling the full story involved people who might prefer the history remain buried lest shame and grief engulf them all over again. And I needed strength and courage to listen to the painful recounting, lest my own heart turn to stone in reaction. To help me stay soft and open, I repeated a mantra often during my work:

I believe in the transformative power of love.
Block out all other voices in my head and listen only for the voice of love.
Let the voice of love fill my heart and melt the ice.
I believe in the transformative power of love that works through me.
I believe in the transformative power of love that works through others.
Keep me listening for the voice of love.
Bathe my heart in the warmth of love.
Keep my heart warm, not cold.

This mantra of love was especially important as I struggled to know what to call the event. The bombing? The murder? The tragedy? The unimaginable thing that happened for which no explanation seemed adequate? I ended up calling it "the event" in most instances. It helped me to keep my emotions in check and move forward with painful detail.

I struggled with knowing I would have to learn more about the man who carried the bomb. Up until now, he was a one-liner to me in fifty years of prolific conversation about everything except this event. I had not even remembered his name. I had never learned to hate this man, but it seemed wrong, even now, to get to know him. Yet I needed to know who he was, his background, his story, for me to get any satisfaction to the answer of "Why?"

No matter what I learned, I certainly didn't want to cast him in a light to be envied or admired. I didn't want to know him in any way that might soften me to his deed. Yet, unless I wanted my heart to harden, I had to allow the transformational power of love to be my guide as I got to know him. I came to accept that I had to listen to both the good and the bad about him, and come to terms that he might have been both.

What should I call him in this story? Criminal? Murderer? The Devil? These words seemed too dastardly, too wicked, almost too smart. "Crazy" seemed the most fitting; after all, he seemed to have lost connection with reality; and he planned and carried out something that had bigger consequences than he ever seemed to have contemplated. But even crazy seemed apologetic. Finally, I decided just to call him by his last name, Holbrook.

When I started this project, I found that I was not alone in the mistaken belief that his wife had also died in the event. In addition, before I began interviewing people, I had never realized that Holbrook had children. But as I pieced together the "players" in this tragedy, those who had been affected, I found that Holbrook had been married for twenty years, and had three, mostly grown children at the time.

Another common thought among people I spoke with was that, of course, the man's family would have left the area by now. They would have been catastrophically shamed. Guilty by association. My fantasy world had them fleeing under the cover of night for fear of revenge or retaliation. They surely wouldn't have wanted to face townspeople every day and be reminded of what their father, husband, son had done.

But the truth is exactly the opposite. The family had mostly stayed in town, in the area. Kept a low profile, but stayed nonetheless, because they, too, were in shock. They, too, were a part of a community. They had ties with friends and neighbors who reached out and held their hands through the ordeal and the aftermath. In fact, I came to realize that their world was rocked and shattered in a way far worse than mine, and worse than the other bystanders of this story. They knew this man, had lived with him, had loved him, had shared his name. No one would ever want to believe that someone they had loved would be capable of such a methodical and horrific lapse in judgment. This was no longer just my story. This was their story, too.

NORMAL

Hillbillies

Bob Temple, former police chief of Circleville, Ohio, started his job in 1959, when I was one year old. He retired in 1988, and on the day I spoke with him, he was eighty-five, bright, alert, memory intact, and still the down-home guy trying for a sense of humor. "I've got one foot in the grave and the other on a banana peel," he said with a twinkle in his eye as we started our conversation.

He was eager to tell me his recollections of that day in 1967, which he considered the worst moment of his career. "It's about time," he said. "Nobody's ever asked before. Long overdue."

He continued with a warning I had not expected: "Before we start, I just want to make one thing clear: Your dad was one of the most upstanding and honorable men in town. No matter the rumors you might hear, he did not have an affair with that woman. 'Those people' were from Kentucky. They just weren't like us."

He had arranged for us to meet privately at Ted Lewis Park, under a pavilion, where bystanders couldn't overhear. He promised to be open and honest. He intended to be graphic. He sat in front of me on a stage, like a performer. As the storyteller, in control, he jumped right in: "I was about forty-five minutes away at Lake White when this happened. It was a Saturday, my day off. But, luckily, we were just docking the boat when I saw a Sheriff's car in the parking lot. They motioned me over and told me my town was on fire. I needed to get back to Circleville. I was on Main Street forty-five minutes later."

It was with a bit of embarrassment that I listened to Chief Temple describe the man who blew up Bingman's Drug Store.

"You have to remember that those people from Kentucky were flooding to Circleville for jobs in the cannery. It was only sixty miles north, so they would come up here, but not change their ways. They were different people; they had different ways."

Chief Temple was describing people from Kentucky who had been moving to Circleville for a century, particularly in the early 1900s and around the time of the great depression. Circleville was one of the booming stops on what was known as the "Hillbilly Highway."[3]

Chief Temple was describing an Appalachian Hillbilly, and the old stereotypes came back to me: Ignorant, back-woods folk who liked their women barefoot and pregnant. Moonshiners and weekend drunkards who liked to get into brawls and smash things up. In-bred wife beaters with no gumption. "Those people" were branded by the TV series "Hee Haw," dressed in overalls and missing teeth, known for their love of the Grand Ole Opry and hootenannies, and living in pigeon-ridge-poverty or low-lying hollers. And they talked with a thick, pregnant, hillbilly accent.

A lot of people in Ohio pride themselves on being above that, cosmopolitan by comparison. But those airs hide the truth that most Ohioans have more than a foothold in Appalachia. Ohioans came from somewhere, and looking around, we might find that many more than we think swam across the Ohio River. It pops out when some of the prettiest, most cultured-looking women in Ohio open their mouth and out comes a hillbilly twang. It's shocking when you haven't been around it for a while.

All of that went through my head as I listened to Chief go on about "those people".

I was embarrassed, too, because even though I have shaken the accent, I was keenly aware that he could have been talking about my family. I, too, have one foot in the hills and one foot in the city. My people came from down there and the backwoods. When asked about my heritage, I have often said that my people crawled out from under a rock in West Virginia and made their way out of the hills to Portsmouth. We are a *Heinz 57* blend of eastern and western European lines with no present-day ties to the motherland.

My great-grandfather on my mom's side ran the company store at the coal mine in Nolan, West Virginia. Back in the day, if you sat around one of the family reunions held out at the old homestead farm outside of Portsmouth, watching the uncles and aunts play penny-ante poker, sipping whiskey, chugging beers, and telling tales, you would have learned that we were related by a not-so-distant tattered family thread to the Hatfields, who led the famous feud with the McCoys. In fact, my grandmother had worked for one of the West Virginia Hatfields as a teenager, from which she earned her family nickname "Nanny." She, too, left the backwoods of West Virginia at the age of eighteen and headed for the big city of Portsmouth to find her fortune and a husband.

At the turn of the twentieth century, Portsmouth was one of the first stops on the Hillbilly Highway. It was the most important city between Cincinnati and Pittsburg, with train tracks, a canal, and the confluence of the Scioto and Ohio Rivers transporting goods in three directions. In the early 1900s, Portsmouth was a manufacturing town, the fourth-largest city in the world for making shoes. In addition, there were factories that made bricks, steel, furniture, engines and a hundred other items. At the height of the boom, steel mills and coal trains made the town gritty and bustling.

My family was squarely a part of this boom. My maternal grandmother worked in a shoe factory and my paternal grandfather worked in a steel mill. However, by the time I knew

Portsmouth in the 1960s, my parents had long escaped, the steel mills were almost all closed, and the region had a very old and tired feeling, just like my grandparents, who we visited frequently.

My mom, with her maiden name of Eileen Morgan, grew up mainly in the City of Portsmouth. My mom's family had it rough during the Great Depression and traveled the Hillbilly Highway all the way to Michigan looking for work. They happily returned to Portsmouth a few years later, once my grandpa was called back to his job on the railroad. In the good old days, the train would pass by just a few blocks from my mom's house, stop, and let my grandpa off or on, depending on the time of day. The sound of a train whistle was music to my family.

My dad, Teddy Lee Foster, was an only child who grew up in an eastern neighborhood of Portsmouth called Sciotoville, on the north bank of the Ohio River. My dad could look out his bedroom window and see the river, a wide and muddy expanse that, if local lore had it correct, my dad swam across in his teens on a dare.

What saved my family from being one of "those people" was the consequence of two things: First, much to the delight and pride of my maternal grandparents, their three daughters did not *have to* get married in front of the barrel of a shotgun. We went to the family reunions with our noses in the air for that reason. That, in large part, allowed the second thing to happen.

Both my mom and my dad were able to continue their education past high school, the first generation in either family to do so. My mom, a good girl and bright, talked her father into letting her go on her own to a nursing school run by Catholic nuns in Huntington, West Virginia. Huntington is about sixty miles east of Portsmouth, in the heart of Appalachia. Getting there meant traveling along the Ohio River, wedged between steep mountainsides with "beware of falling rock" signs and the river's meandering shoreline. The nuns provided housing for unaccompanied females, with strict rules and a grueling schedule.

My dad went to college on the G.I. Bill after serving first in Occupied Japan and later in the Korean War. As a one-generation-removed hillbilly, an Army veteran, and a college-educated pharmacist, this kept him from being classified as one of "those people." He was embraced by Circleville society as "one of us." Few people probably knew that he was from Sciotoville, and his parents from a farm before that.

There was something else that Chief Temple said that hit too close to home. He described Holbrook's attitude toward women. "Those people liked their women to look as plain as possible. Those people from Kentucky didn't adopt our ways. Holbrook's wife started to work at Bingman's and the ladies encouraged her to get her hair done and do her nails. He didn't like that. He called it 'dollish.' He didn't want her to work at Bingman's."

I understood a little of that attitude too. I remember black and white photos of my dad sitting in a bar in Japan, in uniform, with his arm around a pretty lady, surrounded by friends, living it up. He was tall at six-foot-four, lanky-handsome, and probably like my brothers -- polite and charming. Yet, my dad had his 1940s ideas of a woman's place: in the home, "barefoot and pregnant," as the saying goes.

My mom and dad met on a blind date after my dad returned from Korea and my mom was back in Portsmouth, a full-fledged nurse working in a doctor's office. On their very first date, my dad spouted off about his experiences in the Army as a medical tech sergeant. He worked around nurses who, far from home in a conflict zone, had built up a confidence and a competency that he couldn't accept. His famous last words on that first date with my mom were, "I would never marry a nurse!" My five-foot-three nurse-mom had him eating crow and wedding cake within a year. My dad retaliated by taking her to tiny Ada, Ohio, where he went to college at Ohio Northern University. He demanded that "no wife of mine will work out of the home," even though my mom had a profession and they were newlywed-poor and struggling to make ends meet. My dad was an only child and he wanted a bushel of kids. My mom obliged him with a fertile environment. And they were happy. Maybe that's where the comparison with Holbrook ends.

A friend of my parents called my mom and my dad "very decisive people." I took that to mean they were both very strong-willed. But they were also outgoing, smart and confident. My mom was from a loving family of women, with enough bad examples of cousins and uncles to know what she wanted and didn't want in her life. She was famous for saying, "If you ever hit me, you better make it good because you won't get a second chance...." And, boy, did we believe her.

The Fosters

My dad was so happy to move to Circleville in 1960. After he graduated from college, he had dragged his growing family to small towns all over Ohio – Williamsburg, Minerva and Somerset – chasing better opportunities to be a pharmacist.

Circleville was a county seat of about 12,000 people in a county with a population of about 40,000, and located thirty miles south of Columbus, the capital of Ohio. You could travel thirty minutes in any direction of Circleville and hit another county seat. Circleville was at the crossroads of geological changes, where the glaciers of the ice age had stopped in their evolution of pushing up dirt to form the hills and mountains of Southern Ohio. South of Circleville you could see the rolling hills that led to Appalachia. Going north and west lay the flat lands of corn fields and pastures.

Established in the early 1800s, Circleville carried a few distinctions. The first was that the town was originally build in a circle following the design of local prehistoric earthworks built by Hopewell Indians. The courthouse was the middle of town, and streets proceeded out like spokes of a wheel that led to the next town in every direction. Crossing the spokes were streets in concentric circles, moving block by block outward from the courthouse. While the town's layout was squared off twenty-five years after the founding, its name stuck, and the original design continues to be studied in most university urban design courses. In 1967, the last house of the original circle was razed to make way for a parking lot.[4]

Little remains today to remind the town of these early formations, except a sign at the city entrance that reads, "...built within a prehistoric circle of earthworks." When I was young, we would pass that sign daily at about forty miles an hour. My life experience in Circleville at the time was connected to the local fishing hole, and my young eyes never reached the end of that sentence. So, I made up my own version and grew up believing that Circleville was built around a prehistoric circle of earth*worms*. What I found throughout this story is that some people get it in their heads that things are a certain way because they've known it that way for such a long time, and there's no convincing them that it might have happened differently.

In the 1960s, Circleville was bustling with industry, partly built around processing farm products and partly in manufacturing and assembling goods for a growing appetite of consumers. It was a small community with big aspirations. While just about every county seat in Ohio held a fall festival, Circleville outdid them all by holding "The Greatest Free Show on Earth," the Circleville Pumpkin Show, every October since the turn of the twentieth century. The town blocked off the downtown streets for four days, held daily parades and crowned a queen, while the fifty or more civic clubs and churches in town tried to outsell each other with every imaginable pumpkin treat.

When we moved to Circleville, it was just the five of us -- my mom and dad, sister, brother, and me. We landed temporarily in an apartment downtown, in the upstairs of an old house on Scioto Street, with the railroad tracks behind us. We were three doors down from Mayor Benny Goodman's store on the corner of Scioto and Main Street, and a short walk halfway up the block to Bingman's Drug Store, located on West Main Street.

My dad knew Benny and everyone else in town because, back in the day, Bingman's Drug Store, like most drug stores in that era, had an old-time soda fountain and lunch counter. Being right downtown, Bingman's was a gathering place for shoppers and businessmen. The store had the "friendly druggist" reputation and was popular despite there being three other drugstores in town.

My dad was a good citizen of Circleville, active in his church, a member of the Rotary Club and American Legion, and a Mason, the centuries-old men's secret society where members swear an oath to not disclose their rituals. It had something to do with pledging to be of good character and concerned with morality and ethics, so I don't know why they were so secretive. Many of the prominent men in town were Masons, including my dad's boss, Charlie Schieber. At age twelve, my sister was invited to join the Rainbow Girls, the youth leadership and service arm of the Masons. She got to go to the Masonic Temple for the meetings and wore a formal gown for an induction ceremony. I was jealous and remember her rubbing it in that I couldn't know what they did because it was a secret.

We didn't live in town very long, probably because my brother Bob was "a bun in the oven" and my family needed more room. We moved to the bucolic subdivision of Knollwood Village, a tightknit community of about forty homes located five miles out of town on the way to Hargus Lake. The subdivision was a string of cul-de-sacs, ranch-style and two-story homes bounded by cornfields and cow pastures. The community sat appropriately enough on a knoll, a small hill, overlooking farms and the beautiful Ohio countryside. Kids were given the run of the entire place. No yard had a fence, and there were common areas, a tennis court and wooded back yards to explore via an extensive network of trails kept up by the thirty or so kids who played outside every day. The parents in the neighborhood had two rules: We could play anywhere in Knollwood, but freedom stopped with the first row of corn. And we had to be home when the street lights came on at dusk.

Our neighbors were doctors and lawyers and lots of engineers who worked at the DuPont plant. Moms stayed home; dads went to work. Moms shared cups of sugar, disciplined each other's kids, and drew straws for carpooling trips into town. It was the era when families were proud to own a car, but it was unusual to own two cars, so husbands and wives figured out ride-sharing plans. The kids played many a game of monkey move-up, kick-the-can, and hide-and-seek. We played with frogs and snakes, climbed trees, and swung on vines yelling like Tarzan. Dads "brought home the bacon," taught their kids how to fish, and on summer holidays organized community cookouts of pancakes and bacon cooked on grills in the open commons.

Three memories of my dad have always stuck with me. He would often come home from work and find my mom in a tizzy, having spent the day with us kids; and he would ask us half seriously and half in jest, "Have you had your spanking today?" or, "Do you need a good switching?" When we were really bad, we were threatened with having to pick our own switch from a tree in the back yard. I never remember being hit out of anger, but we did get disciplined in that traditional way. However, if we had been good, when he came home, at least one of us kids would curl up on his lap as he sat in his favorite chair, smoking a pipe and drinking a long-necked Rolling Rock.

My second memory, and, for the longest time my most enduring memory, of my dad, was how angry he would get trying to get us kids to go to sleep at night. I can still see him standing over my bed with his hands on his hips, legs akimbo, telling me, "Go-to-sleep!" My parents had one tough time because, like popcorn, we would individually test their patience every night, pleading to stay up just a little longer. After we were finally asleep, Dad would frequently spend the rest of the evening out in his woodshop in the garage where he made furniture for our bedrooms, and toy guns and slingshots for our playtime delight.

My third memory of my dad was, at first blush, a beautiful story of a man passing down nature's secrets to his offspring. He told me that you could catch a bird by putting salt on its tail. I would run around the back yard -- possibly for years -- trying to throw salt on a bird's tail until I got big enough to realize that it made no sense. I was only big enough, though, to figure out that if you could get close enough to a bird to get the salt on its tail, you were probably close enough to forget the salt and just reach down and grab it. It took me a few more years to realize I was never going to catch a bird. He and my mom probably sat on the porch in the Adirondack chairs that he built, snickering while they watched me, hoping that all that running around would knock me out quickly that night.

My mom and dad were devoted to their respective widowed mothers. We visited Portsmouth at least twice a month and we spent just about the same amount of time at each grandmas' house during our trip. Truth be told, though, the kids loved to visit Grandma Foster best. She let us roam wild all over her three-story clapboard house. She would take us on long walks along the railroad tracks that crossed the Ohio River, and we would pick blackberries in August from the bushes in the back alley.

My youngest brother, the "accidental" fifth child, was born in 1963. Grandmothers, aunts and uncles, with an assortment of cousins in tow, would visit us and whisper among themselves, "Is Eileen done having children yet?" My mom and dad would just smile with their eyes.

Faithfully, our growing family of seven piled into the "Woodie" every Sunday and went to church and Sunday School. If we were good, we all went to the Blue Ribbon Dairy after services for ice cream cones, scandalously eating dessert before lunch.

These are good memories. Norman Rockwell would have enjoyed hanging out with us and drawing his famous Saturday Evening Post covers from the likeness of my family.

The Willisons

Chuck Willison, husband of Francis Willison who died in the event, was born in the eastern part of Ohio, in Monroe County. Chuck was sixth-generation American and could trace his ancestry back to the mid-1700's. His grandfather fought in the Civil War.

His dad, chasing construction jobs, moved the family to little towns around the area until circumstances took them to Akron, where Chuck graduated from high school.

Francis, his soon-to-be wife, lived on the other side of Akron and went to a different high school. The two met after graduation when Tom, a friend of Chuck's, was dating Francis's girlfriend. Chuck explained it this way: "A friend got a hold of me one day and told me about Francis. He wanted me to date her so we could double-date. So, he took me over to meet her. It was 1949, a Tuesday night, close to November."

At the time, Chuck had a half-way decent job and spent his money on a car, as a lot of young men did. He wanted to show off his 1948 Mercury convertible to Francis. "So, I called her the next day and asked her if I could come over that night and I told her I would bring a buddy of mine, a friend for Audrey, her friend. So, we went over Wednesday night and went for a ride. Probably had the top down in November. Top down with the heater on. I saw her that first week on Tuesday, Wednesday, Friday, and Saturday night." After that, he told her, "I'm not going to be in town for a while." Chuck was going deer hunting with his dad in Pennsylvania. He didn't see her for ten days, but they had another date immediately after he got back.

They dated for the next year and started talking about marriage, but that was 1950, going on 1951, and the Chinese were starting trouble in Korea. Chuck knew he was going to be drafted. He got it into his head that it wasn't right to get married and then get drafted. So, they waited. Chuck joined the Ohio National Guard in October 1950 with some friends so they could ship out together when the time came. "We were sure we would be called up before January into the regular army. But we weren't called until the following fall. I am surprised, now that I think about it, that we didn't get married, but I just knew I was getting called up."

Chuck went to Louisiana for boot camp on January 2, 1951. It wasn't until August that he received orders to go overseas. "In September, I came home and, in a surprising twist, we got married." Francis sweet-talked him into it. Francis was an office manager at the time, working at General Tire and Rubber in Akron. She was smart about money and she was in love with Chuck. She combined her practical business sense with her heart's desire to convince him to marry her before he shipped out. Her reasoning was that he would leave as a private first class but would make corporal quickly and be promoted. She reminded him that he would earn more pay if he were married. "Financially it made sense, so we got married," said Chuck with a smile, remembering the good times. "We were in love. We got married on a Friday night and I left on Monday morning."

Chuck went almost straight to Korea, arriving by ship from Japan, artillery shells falling in, on and around the ship as they landed. "They handed me a rifle and told me to go shoot the Chinese. I was shot at a lot, but I shot back more. I was a hunter, so I was a better shot than they were. I had shells all around me, artillery shells, but never was hit. I thank the Lord every day. I've had people close to me hit with shrapnel from a shell."

He was there just a year, but it was an intense year.

"I can't claim a Purple Heart, but I have a Bronze Star from a battle I was in," said Chuck, who, in fact, received a Bronze Star with Valor for meritorious service in combat.

"I was staff sergeant at the time, in control of a squad. We were positioned in this little grove of woods and our mission was to see to it that the Chinese didn't reach our main line. We ran patrols out from the main line almost every night. One night, we got hit by mortar shells coming in. I got everyone into a foxhole, made sure they were in, and then I got into the foxhole. I knew the sergeant in charge of air strikes. We had a radio, and I called him up and said, 'You know where we are?' He said, 'Yeah.' I said, 'Go two hundred yards at one o'clock from where we were supposed to be.' It wasn't but a few minutes later that five mortars dropped from the sky; we heard five explosions. There was never any movement down there after that. I was scared the commander would say, 'Go down there and see what's going on.' But, instead, he said, 'You took care of it, so come on back in.'"

When Chuck came home, his brother and dad were living in Circleville. They offered to help him find a job there. Francis wasn't eager to move because she liked Akron and had a good job, but Chuck didn't like big towns and, back in 1953, Circleville was a whole lot smaller than it is now. Chuck got a job at Wardell's Carpet and Rugs, which was downtown, right next to Bingman's.

Francis got a job right away at the telephone company, as an office girl, not an operator. Not too much later, she started working for Dean and Grace Bingman at Bingman's Drug Store. She was educated enough to take care of the books. When Charlie Schieber bought the drug store, she stayed on, working for him as a bookkeeper.

Chuck, his brother and father also tried their hand at building houses. They bought some land about five miles out of town on State Route 56, back when it was called Route 4. They built a house on one side of the property to sell, and put up a trailer in the middle of the property where Chuck's family lived while he saved enough money to build their homestead on the other side of the property.

Francis and Chuck's oldest son was born in 1955, followed by two more boys, one right after the other. Francis cut back to part time once she had her hands full with the three boys. "She always worked on Saturdays, and maybe two nights during the week, she'd be gone after supper," said Chuck. "She'd go in and do the bookkeeping and might not get home until ten or eleven o'clock."

Every morning for almost thirteen years, Chuck stopped at Bingman's soda counter for coffee before work. He knew the ladies who worked there. Maybe not by name, but he knew most of the employees by sight. He knew Martha Lagore, who worked at the cosmetic counter, and had talked to her husband a couple of times. Of course, he knew his wife's boss, Charlie Schieber; and he remembered that Charlie's wife, Jean, and his wife frequently exchanged children's clothes. "I didn't know Holbrook, but I knew his wife worked there. I might have spoken to her when I went in to see Francis, but we weren't really acquainted," Chuck said, straining to remember.

Continuing a family tradition dating back five generations, Chuck joined Circleville's fledging Church of Christ congregation. Back in Akron, his mom and dad went to a small Church of Christ. When Chuck was just fifteen, he recalled, "The congregation bought a little building and it didn't have a baptistry. Dad and I built the baptistry and I was baptized in it." Chuck started going to services with his brother in Circleville, when the congregation met downtown in the old Farm Bureau building. Chuck and his brother helped construct the church's first building on Moats Drive; and when the congregation outgrew it, they helped build the church that stands today on North Court Street.

"When I came here in 1953, my brother and his two kids had attended this church for about a year, along with another man and his wife and their two kids. Charles Cochrane, his wife and two daughters came up from Marietta to be the preacher. That was the congregation when we came here. Francis was not a member at that time. Shortly afterward, Bob and his wife and I talked her into joining us," said Chuck.

"We were in love," Chuck remembered of this time in their life. "We both worked to make a good living for the kids. We never fought. We had few disagreements. She might want something one way and I would want it different, but we didn't fight over it. She was just a good-hearted girl."

The Schiebers

L arry Schieber is my age and his dad was my dad's boss. We
went to the same church and our lives as children
intertwined around Sunday School, youth fellowship and choir.
Little did we know that our fathers were destined to become
double headliners in a joint funeral.

Larry's dad, Charlie Schieber, grew up on a farm in Bucyrus,
in northern Ohio. He left to study at Ohio Northern University,
graduated from the College of Pharmacy, and passed the
pharmacy boards in 1949. In 1954, he moved to Circleville, and,
at age thirty-five, purchased his own drug store from Dean
Bingman, the store's namesake. Once Charlie was settled in, he
went home, married his sweetheart, and brought her back to
Circleville. [5]

Mrs. Schieber, the only name I knew her by as a kid, always
had the most beautiful silver-blue hair. (Her secret, her daughter
told me, was *Silk and Silver #16.*) She grew up on a farm outside
of Bucyrus, secured her teaching credential from Heidelberg
College, and taught business courses at the high school near
Bucyrus for ten years. She and Charlie were engaged for many

years, but he delayed getting married until he was financially on his feet, which involved long hours once he bought his own pharmacy. Jean, Mrs. Schieber's proper name, was eager to get married and end the long-distance romance. A few months before they tied the knot, Jean wrote to Charlie about the prospect of marriage and starting a new life in Circleville. "I won't mind being alone in the apartment eight to twelve hours a day since there won't be almost one hundred miles between us."

Once married, Jean, of course, wouldn't work. That was the custom of the day, expected by both the husband and wife. In fact, she wrote Charlie, "It's *such* a relief though to not have to think of going through another year of teaching. I had thought that I would like to make it to ten years of teaching, on account of my retirement money, and since I've made it, I'm <u>more</u> than happy to quit."

She kept up with her profession, as most married but non-working professional women of her day did, by participating in her sorority, the Beta Rho Chapter of Delta Kappa Gamma, which Charlie jokingly called "Alpha Beta *Gamma Globulin*," a reference to a common drug protocol that boosted the human immune system to ward off bacterial infections.

Jean was in her late thirties when she had their son, Larry. The Schiebers were about ten years older than my parents, but Larry and his sister, Karen, were the same age as my younger brother and me. From my youthful point of view, the Schieber family was very straight-laced. Seriously proper. Well behaved. Calm. Not like my wild, savage family. We were rough and tumble with love and dirt getting all over us.

I never remember going to the Schieber's house, but if I did, I can imagine that my young self would have worn my Easter dress, with bonnet and little white gloves, sitting in their parlor with my hands folded in my lap; with sweat dripping off me, fidgeting and distracted by butterflies and flowers outside the window calling me to play.

Larry was in Boy Scouts with my brothers and probably had a sash full of all the hard badges, yet I can imagine that his uniform was always well-fitting, never wrinkled or sullied. This seemed to me a serious house of honest, hardworking, good people.

Larry would never describe his family this way. He remembers being carefree about school, much to the dismay of his mother, the schoolteacher. But he also remembers that they had fun, took great vacations to Florida, and that his parents were devoted to his sister and him. Larry particularly adored and admired his dad, loving to visit the drugstore and sometimes being allowed to ring the register for a customer.

Larry's sister, Karen, has vague memories of her father, because she was only six or seven when he died and her dad put in a lot of hours at the store. "I didn't see my dad very much," she said. "He was very active in Kiwanis, and other civic organizations. He was working a lot."

Charlie did work a lot and was an active and important community leader. His obituary outlined his extensive involvements:

> "...member of the Circleville First Methodist Church, the Kiwanis Club, past president of the Circleville Area Chamber of Commerce, the local Masonic Chapter Council, Commander and Shrine, member of the board of directors of the Circleville Parking Lot Corporation, the Pickaway Country Club and the Ohio State Pharmacists Association.[6]

My dad was also involved in many of the same organizations, mainly because Charlie invited him and encouraged him to be a good citizen. In fact, they were seen so often together that many people told me that my dad and Charlie were good friends, with a similar sense of humor and love of fun.

Karen shared with me a few fond memories of her dad. "I remember standing on his feet as he walked me to bed at night and he let me sit with him on the riding mower when he mowed the lawn," she said. Her dad also smoked a pipe, a smell she loves to this day.

"We would go on Sunday drives, often to Bucyrus to visit grandmother. It was the time before seat belts and my dad made a wooden platform to go over the hump in the back seat of the car so Larry could stretch out and sleep; and I would stretch out above him on the seat. I also remember that we would go over hills on our trips where, if you went fast enough, you could almost feel like you were airborne. Larry and I would chant together, 'Daddy go fast!' and we would fly over the hills, leaving our stomachs in the air, much to our delight." Karen recalled that her dad was funny, a practical joker, and had a great sense of humor.

They had a cottage out on Hargus Lake, near our house, that Larry and Karen both remembered fondly from their family outings. A few months before the event, perhaps in an ominous premonition, an unseasonal February funnel cloud blew through the area. It touched down, first in our back yard, knocking a big old tree across the road. It landed next, with precision, five miles away, hitting the middle of three houses built right next to each other, destroying the Schieber's cottage. The funnel cloud picked up the roof of their cottage, dropped it several feet away, and all four walls collapsed inward. There was nothing left but the foundation; and yet the neighboring two houses were completely untouched.[7]

Bingman's

Bingman's Drug Store was located on iconic Main Street, about a half-block from the center of town. Dean Bingman bought the store in 1953. Formerly one of two Rexall Drugs in Circleville, he changed the store name to Bingman's and began building his reputation as "the friendly pharmacist."

Charlie Schieber came along the next year and bought the drug store from Dean. Dean provided the financing for the inventory and transferred his store lease to Charlie. In consideration, he continued working at Bingman's and worked with Charlie for the next decade to create the best family pharmacy in town.[8] Charlie saw no reason to change the store name, so folks might have been confused about who the proprietor was until Dean retired in 1965. Both men worked hard to build the store's name and reputation, and it showed through their customers' loyalty. Bingman's did well despite competition from chain drug stores that were starting to open in Circleville.

The store rented space on the first floor, at street level, in a typical downtown three-story brick building with apartments on the second and third floors. Wardell Carpet and Rug Store was on one side; a liquor store, on the other and J.C. Penney, across the street. As typical in Ohio towns, back alleys crisscrossed through the middle of each city block.

Bingman's was more than a drug store; it was stuffed to the gills with merchandise, more like a variety store with a pharmacy in the back. The biggest draw for folks, as I have said, was the soda fountain and lunch counter. Bingman's was a hangout for young and old, where you could find the Mayor, local businessmen, and high school teenagers alike sitting at the counter on red vinyl stools or in wooden booths, ordering milkshakes and cheeseburgers. Many people came just to hang out at Bingman's, to browse the store and "be seen." My sister's favorite part of the store was the magazine rack. She and her friends would drool over the pictures and stories of The Monkees and the Beatles, and dogear the top copy of Teen Magazines to learn the latest secrets for applying makeup and kissing boys.

By 1966, there were three other competing pharmacies in Circleville. So, on his own, after Mr. Bingman retired, Charlie wanted to "expand the shopping pleasure" of his customers and decided to modernize the store, investing upwards of $40,000 – a significant outlay in those days. The renovations were completed in February 1967, just a few months before it wouldn't matter. The grand celebration of the remodeling was written up in the newspaper with pictures and a half-page article explaining that the store "modernized" with an "accent on 'self-selection' and other customer conveniences," but kept sufficient staff to provide "personal patron service."[9] Times were changing, and Bingman's was keeping up.

Every department was updated. At the front door, a new check-out counter greeted customers. An expanded cosmetics section ran along the wall on the left side when you walked in and included a "cosmetics bar complete with two seats for the convenience of the ladies who like to study name brand products in detail." Furthermore, the newspaper proclaimed, "male customers have not been forgotten either. A section accenting shaving creams, lotions, and other needs are located opposite the cosmetic area." In addition, the store added a camera section selling equipment and accessories, an "expanded are(a) for greeting cards, stationery and school supplies," and a candy counter with "an exclusive brand that ships a fresh supply" to the store each week. The store even had a section dedicated to animal health and filled veterinary prescriptions for large and small animals. Of course, the lunch counter and seating had been remodeled and expanded in line with its popularity.

The prescription area began half way to the back of the store. Customers could be greeted at the prescription check-out counter by the attendant on duty, review the shelves behind the attendant full of "over the counter" drugs on the shoulder-high half-wall, and look over the wall to see the heads and shoulders of pharmacists in their sparkling white smocks, standing in their well-lighted, white and clean-looking pharmacy space, bent over their work, counting pills and compounding prescriptions. The pharmacy area was elevated by a step or more so that the pharmacists looked out royally over the floor of merchandise. Above their heads was a big sign reminding customers that this was the PRESCRIPTIONS area. Behind the men in white were rows of shelves holding labeled bottles, new "indexed drug cabinets for prescription files, a biological refrigerator and a complete line of pharmaceuticals."

The store renovations also carved out a narrow hallway to the right of the prescriptions counter. It led to an office, a small receiving area and a new back door for customers and deliveries (and, ironically, also providing a supposed fire exit), with three or four parking spaces in the alley.

In the middle of the store was an open stairway leading to the basement that, in bygone days, provided room for additional shopping. During the renovation, the stairs were roped off and the basement was used mainly for storing stock.

Bingman's must have been a great place to work. At the beginning of 1967, the store employed twenty-one people, including three pharmacists.[10] Many of the staff had worked there forever. I know this because every New Year's Eve,

Bingman's took out a three-quarter page ad in the local paper thanking the community for its patronage and listing all the employees. It was part of the advertising that made Bingman's personal. Everyone in town knew the employees by their first name. That and the fact that Bingman's was a proud sponsor of a consistently strong Little League team in a town that loved baseball.

The store was staffed with at least five people at any one time: one at the front register, either Mrs. Lagore or Mrs. Holbrook at the cosmetic counter, at least one of the three druggists in the pharmacy area; at least one but sometimes up to seven women working in the popular soda fountain and lunch counter, and a stock boy or two who could fill in when and where needed.

Of the four employees who would eventually die in the store, my dad was the last to come on board, at the end of 1960. So, for at least seven years, the main characters of this story were long-time friends and colleagues.

My dad was known as a "good-guy druggist" who went above and beyond. For instance, former co-workers said, he was known to "brown bag" the little old ladies, meaning he would ask elderly customers to bring all their prescriptions in so he could check for unintended drug interactions. He was also known as a family man. Employees said that when my mom would come into the store, dad would drop everything. "Your mom would come in like a whirlwind, always joking and speaking to everyone. She would often have her kids in tow and her kids' friends in tow." No one was quite sure how many kids they had, but the consensus was that they could field a small baseball team, at least.

Martha Lagore, or "Mart," as she was known by family and friends, was the perfect saleswoman for the cosmetic counter. Customers asked for her by name to help them look and smell as well-put-together as she appeared. It was thought that she came from a well-heeled family because she was always dressed like a million dollars, with never a hair out of place, makeup expertly applied, and wearing stockings that had a seam up the back. Truth be told, she was a local girl who had grown up on the south side of town and who had eloped at seventeen to marry her sweetheart, much to the dismay of her devoted family.

She started working at the drug store when her youngest child married, had babies of her own and moved away. The order that those things happened is not important, except to say Mart worked mainly to earn a little money to send to her daughter and grandchildren.

Her husband worked at the local paper mill. To the public, the couple seemed madly in love. He was very attentive to her. To her family, it was her husband who insisted that Mart maintain her pristine appearance. He was compulsive about that. He needed everything to be just right and he could be fiercely obsessive.

Francis Willison, as mentioned, had worked for more than a decade, part-time, as Bingman's bookkeeper and came in on Saturdays to do payroll. She was quiet when she was in the office and seldom seen, working as she did in the back office, down the hallway, near the exit.

Bob Scranton, the third pharmacist at the time, was a protégé of Charlie and Dean. Bob was a stock boy, still in high school, the year Charlie came to Circleville. Bob continued to work at the store during summers while at pharmacy school at Ohio Northern University; he was promoted to pharmacist when he passed the State Boards in 1964.[11]

In 1967, the stock boys were Scott Lindsay and Joe Tomlinson. Joe was sixteen and fairly new. He was being trained by Scott to take over when Scott left for college in the fall.

Scott's plans had always been to go to pharmacy school at Charlie, Ted and Bob's alma mater, Ohio Northern University. In fact, Charlie saw Scott's potential and had offered to sponsor him with a loan to pay for school. Joe, on the other hand, got the stock boy job because he had impressed Charlie with his reliability as a paper boy. The Schiebers had been great customers and big tippers on Joe's paper route.

Phyllis Holbrook began working at Bingman's sometime in 1964.[12] She was attractive, petite with dark hair, nice and friendly. She liked Bingman's because it accommodated working parents. They might let the female employees come in late after getting their kids off to school, or take off at lunchtime to go home to fix the kids' lunch or let them leave when school got out. Phyllis had that kind of schedule, and she appreciated it.

She worked all over the store but particularly liked working near the cosmetic counter with Mart. Phyllis and Mart were friends. They had a lot in common, like the difficulties of being married women who worked in public in a small town. It could be tough on a marriage. Mart's husband would pick her up from work every night, to make sure his wife made it home safely, with reputation intact. The couple often gave Phyllis a ride home, too, since they lived only a few blocks apart, on opposite ends of Mill Street. Mart knew about Phyllis's domestic problems as she had once helped Phyllis cover up a bruised and blackened eye at the cosmetic counter. After Phyllis filed for divorce,[13] dropping her off at night included a ritual to make sure Phyllis's husband wasn't lurking around; and for that friendship, the Lagores were on Holbrook's bad side.

The Holbrooks

I started writing this story wondering how I was going to delve into the lives of complete strangers, people I wasn't sure I even wanted to know. I had no background on the Holbrook family. I knew vaguely where the family had lived at the time of the event: on the other side of town from where I grew up, in a working class and sometimes rough neighborhood. I asked around, but no one I knew could tell me anything about them, about the kids now all grown up. I snooped around the Internet and found names and addresses. I simply looked in the phone book and found the phone numbers. My imagination considered all the scenarios of how this family might react to me calling them out of the blue. I went, "Eeny, Meeny, Miny, Moe" and decided to call the oldest son, Arnold. I worried for weeks about calling him; when I finally did, I got a stress headache as soon as Edie, his wife, answered the phone.

"Edie, do you have a minute to talk? …my father was killed in the event…."

To my surprise, Edie, or Edith, which is her proper name, listened very kindly, and in a thoughtful and calm way said, "It would be a very good idea for Arnold to talk to you. Come to our house on Friday at 11 a.m…."

So there I was, about to meet the family of the man whose handiwork had changed everything. I was scared to go to their house; I didn't know what to expect.

Arnold and Edie lived not too far from where he grew up, in an older part of town with small one- and two-story vinyl-sided houses built in the 1940s for factory workers and their families. A neighborhood where trailer-court poverty was tucked in behind the thin veneer of everything-is-OK. Their street was right on the edge of town, where cracked sidewalks disappeared into the roadway, not the raised sidewalks, curbs and gutters of our fancy subdivision. Many things could be going on behind the front doors in this neighborhood, I thought, and I was afraid of what this one door might reveal.

Edie answered the door. She was sweet-looking, probably my age. Medium height and a mature figure. Just the way we women age. She sat back down on her recliner and showed me the "baby" on her lap, a new toy-sized puppy she was cuddling in a blanket to keep warm. She introduced me to her pup and chatted for a few minutes about nothing, as if we were old friends. She didn't seem nervous at all. After a few minutes, she offered, "Have a seat. I'll go get Arnold. He's lying down."

I had a few minutes to look around as I waited. Just like many folks in Circleville, Arnold and Edie had converted their front porch into a closed-in sitting room that they could use even in the dead of winter. Furnished with two reclining chairs and a glider, the room's big, bright windows allowed them to monitor the happenings on the street. Surprisingly absent, given how much time they probably spent here, was a television. The porch-room was clean and clutter-free.

I was nervous because I still didn't know what to expect of Arnold. I had never laid eyes on a Holbrook, not even a picture, and neither Edie nor the house gave me any clues. Were these men big and burly? Were they mean? Curt? Aggressive? Foolish? Arnold came out and -- surprise -- he looked just like a regular guy. Regular sized. Regular personality. Cordial. He didn't look his seventy-one years; he looked more like a kid who had grown up. He was wearing sweat pants and a T-shirt, and seemed to be in decent shape. Probably looked just like he did in high school. I finally relaxed a bit, feeling comfortable in these surroundings and with these people.

I asked Arnold if I could record our conversation and he said yes. I showed him my phone app for recording and he seemed tickled with the technology. "State your name," I asked into the microphone and handed the phone to him. He took it hesitantly, maybe embarrassed or shy, but quickly he was lost in the instructions.

"Arnold. A-R-N-O-L-D Holbrook," he spelled directly into the phone. "Take down just the basic information. Just the facts ma'am," he played around. He added a nervous laugh as he handed it back to me.

"No, I'll need more than that," I responded, also with a bit of a nervous laugh.

I started by saying, "I was nine years old at the time. But being nine, I learned just this much about what happened." I held my two fingers close together. "And that was all I ever knew."

Arnold responded to me, "You just knew your father was killed in an accident and that was it."

"Well, maybe a little more…" I replied.

Arnold jumped right in and to the point. "I don't know what they told you over the years, but he was going to kill my mother. He knew she was at home. I suspected that my dad thought my mother was having an affair with someone at the drugstore. And he was going to do away with him."

There. The rumors were on the table. I immediately jumped in. "Do you hold any stock to the stories that your mom was having an affair?" I asked. I couldn't believe we were at the "punch line" so quickly.

Arnold responded quietly. "I just couldn't believe it. I don't think she was, to tell you the truth. I don't think she was."

Arnold spoke with a Southern Ohio twang, but he also had his own distinct way of talking. It was almost like he had a big marble in his mouth that forced him to enunciate each and every word. The words came out clearly, but slightly distorted. Edie told me he was a bit hard of hearing, so that might be behind this inflection.

He seemed relaxed and willing to talk, but he smiled a lot, which gave me the impression that, underneath, he was probably as nervous as I was. He was prepared to talk to me and he seemed at ease in his recliner with his feet up. The chair was pointed at an angle so he didn't have to talk eye to eye with me. He also had to adjust the AC unit on the wall behind his head because he couldn't hear with it going full blast.

As time went on, I realized he was a master storyteller, with modulations and suspense in the right places, and a hesitancy or stutter to get other words out. Strong, baritone voice, almost sounding like Popeye with his *errs* and *ummms* and *ahhs*. I could shut my eyes and see a pipe hanging from the corner of his mouth as he told me his story.

[]

Arnold's father, Lee Holbrook, was born and half-way raised deep in Kentucky. His family came from Old Kentucky. Appalachia. His parents had a twenty-acre farm in a place called Irish Creek, right next to California Holler. The closest town was Louisa, Kentucky, or Lu-EYE-za as they called it down there, located on the banks of the Big Sandy River, the border between Kentucky and West Virginia. The highway twisted through a valley, with hills -- mountains to some -- on both sides. Everyone either lived up in the hills or down in the hollers; there was no such thing as flat land in that part of Kentucky.

"Down there, if you had a twenty-acre farm, ten of it was on the side of a hill. The only way to make a living was to put out a "tabacca" patch and work it hard to get the most dollars per square acre that you could get. You either planted tobacco or found a spot to run off some moonshine. If it weren't for those two options, people down there would have starved to death. That's why there's so many Kentuckians in Ohio: they damn near starved to death in the hills," Arnold said.

During the Depression, Holbrook's parents packed up their family and went north on Route 23, the Hillbilly Highway. They settled in the country near Circleville, on a farm near Williamsport, by what is now Deer Creek Reservoir.

Holbrook graduated from high school in 1942 and then joined the Navy when he was eighteen or nineteen, during the height of World War II. "When my dad went into the Navy, he was fresh off the farm. If someone wanted to know my dad's Social Security number, why, he didn't have one!" exclaimed Arnold. "He probably didn't have a Social Security number until he got out of the Navy." While that may not be technically true, it was Arnold's way of emphasizing his dad's limited connection to the ways of the world.

In the Navy, Holbrook was a cop, an MP, as military police are known, on board a ship. He wasn't in the Navy for long. "He fell down in the hold of a ship and hurt his back and they mustered him out pretty quickly," said Arnold. "I heard the stories that dad was a demolition expert and I thought 'bull-crap,' no way." (This was a misinformed detail repeated in newspaper articles about the event, trying to explain how Holbrook knew how to make a bomb.)

After he got out of the Navy, Holbrook took a job as a cop in Circleville for about two years, but he didn't like the work -- it didn't pay much either -- and he quit. Police Chief Temple had heard about Holbrook's time as a local police officer and said bluntly about him, "He was a crazy man. He was fired for shooting birds out of trees in the middle of town. That's how *those people* were." Holbrook had lived in Ohio for close to thirty years, yet he was still considered an outsider by community leaders.

Young Phyllis McDonald was raised on a farm halfway between Circleville and Williamsport. She was still in high school when she started dating Holbrook. Phyllis was maybe sixteen, and Holbrook was back from the Navy and working as a cop when Phyllis got pregnant. They married in July 1945, moved to Circleville, and Arnold came along in September, "premature."[14]

"Back in those days," Arnold said, "if a girl got pregnant and she wasn't married, they would give her a bus ticket out of town. She would run to the big city. Or word-of- mouth passed around that she could go to ole' so-and-so's house and they would finish raising her up and help with the kid. You've heard of shotgun weddings? There were a lot of them back then. Pappa would go over to the boy's house with his shotgun and say, 'You *will* marry my daughter or I'll blow your brains out.' Nowadays, nobody thinks anything of it. If a girl has a baby, doesn't get married, so what? Back then, it was a whole different world.

"That's one thing that kind of ate on my dad, that they had to get married. That he was tied down. He thought he could have done a lot better if he didn't have to marry my mom," said Arnold, sadly.

After the first baby came (Arnold), Holbrook got a job at the local feed mill. Within two years, Phyllis gave birth to a daughter, and four years later they had a son. However, there was early evidence of discontent in their marriage. Holbrook separated from Phyllis for a short time in 1947, just two years after they married, and filed for divorce, swearing that she was "quarrelsome" and that "she refused to cook his meals."[15] She retaliated and sued him for non-support of two minor children.[16]

"He had a horrible dead-end job at the feed mill, carrying bags of dog food around. He was a common laborer, something you could teach a monkey to do," said Arnold. The mill eventually burned down in 2008, but it was a fire trap even back then. "The only thing that kept it from burning down years ago," Arnold said, "was all the sweat spilled in the place." Arnold, too, had worked for thirty years in a factory, and so he may have identified too closely with what he thought his father's mindless and soul-crushing job must have been like.

But that's how it was back then. Circleville had the factory jobs and the unemployment rate was low. "I don't think Circleville even had a welfare department, unemployment was so low," Arnold exaggerated. But that didn't mean people were satisfied or content with their jobs.

Holbrook didn't want his wife to work outside of the home, and Phyllis would have preferred to have stayed home, but she worked to make ends meet. She worked in restaurants, first at the Wardell Party Home and then at the Pickaway Arms, both popular Circleville establishments that hosted civic club lunches and important dinner parties. She worked a split shift, going in at eleven in the morning, coming home at two in the afternoon, and then returning by five for the dinner shift.

"At Pickaway Arms, my mom worked for practically nothing," said Arnold, "maybe twenty-five cents an hour plus tips." Yet one of the greatest perks was that, with her four or five dollars in tips, she was allowed to buy all of the leftover food each day. "She would clean out the refrigerator, taking a piece of this and a piece of that, two pieces of pie, two pieces of cake. She would even drain the coffee pot and bring it home. Everything at the restaurant was homemade, made fresh every day, including the bread. The only thing that was not made at that restaurant was the ice cream." Arnold continued: "You could go in there and buy yourself a fine meal for two dollars and ninety-five cents, which in the 1960s would be twenty or thirty bucks now." And Arnold smiled as he remembered, "The food was fantastic."

While working, Phyllis met all kinds of people, first at the restaurants and later at Bingman's Drug Store. "Over the years, she got to know all these people, the city wheels, the big shots, judges and lawyers and 'Indian chiefs'; the big, rich guys, you know. She got to meet all those people and I got to meet a lot of them, too, when I was growing up," said Arnold. "Now at seventy-one (years old), I know all the big shots in town because I went to school with them."

Then, as now, Circleville was a small town with an unmistakable social strata. Town folk were overly conscious about who they rubbed shoulders with, especially if they could be seen with people multiple rungs up the social ladder. This was important to Phyllis. She was trying to better her position. "My dad was a good old boy from Kentucky and my mom wanted to be the banker's daughter, the rich socialite," said Arnold.

Phyllis and Holbrook would fight about these types of things. For example, "if he was going to get a car, he wanted something he could go fishing in. He had a crummy car, an old 1960 dirty brown Chevy with tail fins on the back and holes in the floor boards; an old clunker. My mom didn't like that, she wanted a fancy, shiny car. My dad didn't care, he just wanted wheels on it.

"My mom wanted tea and crumpets; my dad, just give him a good chaw of tobacco and he was happy. My mom wanted to go out for Champaign at a ballroom; my dad just wanted to go fishing. They didn't fit. It was a combination that didn't work.

It probably bothered Holbrook immensely that his wife was so well known around the city, especially by the professional set, who were mainly men at the time. "My dad had a horrible,

horrible temper," Arnold said. "My dad must have been kind of jealous. If she was to talk to another man, it kind of rubbed him the wrong way. That was his woman and you weren't supposed to talk to her. Things were like that back then.

To put this in context, this was an era of confusing and transitioning roles for women (and men). World War II had called women to duty, to take essential jobs while their men went to war. Once soldiers returned, husbands and wives returned to "normal" life. The women were generally happy to go back into the home and raise the family. But after the kids were grown, these same housewives were not quite as content as before. By the 1960s, women were increasingly working outside of the home, bringing home a paycheck. Women in the working world received encouragement from their co-workers, from other women stepping out of the house. Gradually, and not without conflict, women were not quite as submissive to their husbands' sense of social order. Women in Circleville weren't necessarily "burning their bras" in protest, but they were part of this subtle shift.

"Mom was just mom. She was friendly and outgoing, but she could also be picky and demanding, and that sort of rubbed some people the wrong way, too," Arnold said.

"My dad was just the opposite. He didn't give a damn what you thought of him. He was more down-to-earth. When I was a little kid, I can remember, my dad was a great guy. And then he started drinking. I don't know when it started. When he got a couple of drinks in him, he wanted to kill everybody. He would beat me up and beat mom up and beat my sister up. He was not a happy drunk; he was a mean drunk," Arnold said.

Holbrook was known to get drunk on Friday night and stay drunk till Sunday. His father would come home in drunken rages. Arnold's mom and dad would argue. Holbrook was known to keep a butcher knife under the bed sheets and would threatened to kill Phyllis in her sleep. "She went to bed with him many a night not knowing if she would wake up the next morning," Arnold said. "I dreaded to see the weekends come. I knew my dad would come home stinking rotten drunk. And broke."

Holbrook may have beat the hell out of Arnold, his mom and his sister, but Arnold swore his dad never touched his younger brother, who had health problems, a birth deformity that required multiple surgeries to correct. "My brother was handicapped and my father laid off him. In fact, the two were buddies, my dad and my little brother." Holbrook was a leader in his younger son's Cub Scout troop and a coach for his Little League baseball team, sponsored by Bingman's Drug Store. "I found out more about my father after he was dead than I knew when he was living, from other people. He was a pretty nice fella. He was a friend to everyone except my mom…and me."

I gathered from people I spoke with that friends either liked Holbrook or they liked Phyllis, but not many people liked them both. Holbrook's friends were probably guys from work, his drinking buddies. Guys who may have been as frustrated with life and dealing with similar problems in the struggle to keep their wives in line, dependent and obedient.

The Holbrook house was at the east end of Mill Street, right next to the railroad tracks and right across the street from the feed mill where Holbrook worked. Arnold was a "townie," a kid who lived downtown and ran all over town as if it were his own back yard. He hung out as much as possible downtown because he didn't want to be at home in all that "mess."

Circleville was a bustling town in the 1960s, with a lot for kids to do. It had two bowling alleys, a skating rink and pool hall, two swimming pools, two drive-in movie theaters, and two movie houses. Arnold had all the details about the place: "There were two drive-ins in Circleville. The one called the North Drive-In, was north on the way to Route 23. That's where they showed the B movies: B for bad. At the Starlight Drive-In, they showed the movies after the movie theaters got done with them. We had the Grand Theatre, which was formerly the old Opera House. A real honest-to-God opera house in Circleville! If you saw a movie at the Grand Theatre, you probably saw it a year after it came out in Columbus.

"Downtown Court and Main, where the bank sits now, and before that it was the round bank. We had a youth canteen on the second floor of the bank. It was a place for kids to hang out. We had a ping-pong table, a pool table, a Coke machine and the world's loudest jukebox.

"I can remember the five-and-dime store. You walked in and the first thing you smelled was fresh, roasted peanuts. And Lord knows what kind of candy they had. They sold it by the scoop. You could buy a pair of blue jeans in the basement for a dollar ninety-nine. Every drug store had a soda fountain. You could get a real honest-to-God soda with real honest-to-God ice cream, and you could buy a Coke for six cents in a six-ounce bottle. Half the stores in town had a Coke machine sitting on the sidewalk and you stood by the Coke machine and drank it because you had to give the bottle back."

As Arnold turned into a teenager, he had his own life out of the house and his own group of friends. It was the 1960s after all, a turbulent time in the whole country. The Vietnam War was raging, Kennedy had been shot, desegregation was a "thing," and President Johnson had declared a war on poverty. People often said that Circleville was ten years behind the rest of the world, and while local teenagers didn't seem much caught up in world politics of the time, they liked the music and the parties. Like many teenagers in that day, Arnold and the gang smoked and drank. They had to try it. Arnold was a year older than his friends, and he had a draft card. Draft didn't mean Army. In 1963, it meant being able to buy beer. So Arnold was the popular guy who bought the beer for his friends, and, on top of that, he never got called to military service.

Arnold got married a year after he completed high school and remembers that marriage was his ticket out of the insanity at home. Arnold and his bride were under the age of consent (which was twenty-one at the time), and Arnold's mother didn't want him to marry, so they eloped to Virginia. When they returned, they found an apartment on the other side of downtown, on Scioto Street, and Arnold got a job at Jenkin's Sunoco Station. Arnold stopped going to his parent's house for a good long time. "I stayed away from the house and I wanted nothing to do with it. I got married, ran away and I did *not* go back for a good long time. I knew Mom and Dad were having their quarrels and their fights and I knew that Dad was drunk and broke." He would visit his mother regularly at Bingman's, which was right around the corner from his apartment, but he rarely went to the house.

Phyllis filed for divorce exactly one month before the event, on March 15, 1967, a fact that was made public in the local newspaper. Holbrook was forty, Phyllis was thirty-eight, and they had been married more than twenty years. Arnold heard that his dad wasn't taking it very well, which was something of a mystery to Arnold because he felt sure they hated each other. "When my mom sued him for divorce, he just went crazy. This was long before such a thing as no-fault divorce; and when you got sued for divorce, you had to leave. He was ordered out of the house by the Sheriff."

Holbrook moved into a little motel on the north side of town, the Danny Lee Motel behind a popular carryout, Gourmet Corners, on North Court Street, a mile from downtown. He was not happy. He was not suited to bachelorhood. He was used to having home-cooked meals and sleeping in his own bed, and he suddenly found himself kicked out of his own house. With his dad out of the house, though, Arnold started going around again to see his mom. That's how he happened to be at her home on that particular Saturday in April.

WHAT HAPPENED

The italicized quotations at the beginning of chapters in this section are direct quotations from headlines and newspaper articles at the time, unless otherwise noted.

Saturday, April 15, 1967

To some people, it seemed the world had come to an end. A peaceful Saturday afternoon for about thirty people in Bingman's Drug Store quickly turned into a nightmare.[17]

A feed mill employee, despondent over his failing marriage, dynamited a downtown drug store in Circleville Ohio on Saturday...[18]

The explosion set off a blaze that destroyed three downtown buildings, probably causing hundreds of thousands of dollars in damages. The explosion and fire of tremendous proportion that followed claimed at least five lives, destroyed three downtown businesses and numerous upper level apartments and left the community grief-stricken.[19]

On Saturday, April 15, besides all that was going on in Circleville, Ohio, it was also Income Tax Day for the country. Every year on this day, as I prepare my own returns, I am obliged to remember the twin anniversaries.

On the same day, in the same year, the world was also in upheaval as thousands marched in Washington, New York and San Francisco protesting the Vietnam War and demanding civil rights for blacks. While a bomb was exploding in Ohio, police estimated that 125,000 people listened to a speech by Martin Luther King in front of the United Nations as he took a radical and controversial stand to oppose the Vietnam War. "Over the past two years, as I have moved to break the betrayal of my own silence and to speak from the burning of my own heart, as I have called for radical departures from the destruction of Vietnam, *many persons have questioned me about the wisdom of my path....*"[20] MLK was talking about the dangers of speaking up about controversial things, about getting into the middle of things instead of turning away. Less than a year later MLK would be dead. Yet, on the same day that MLK spoke out, my dad and others in Circleville faced the same dilemma.

On that particular day, a little over fifty years before, the *unsinkable* Titanic hit an iceberg and sank in the icy waters of the North Atlantic on its maiden voyage, killing over fifteen hundred people. That which was deemed impossible, had happened. The sailors were no more prepared than the folks in Circleville for their respective catastrophes. The ship carried less than half the life boats the passengers needed.

On the same day in 1865, President Abraham Lincoln, the sixteenth president of the United States died from an assassin's bullet, shot by John Wilkes Booth at Ford's Theater in Washington, D.C., the night before. Lincoln represented high integrity and moral fiber. My dad and Charlie Schieber could also be described that way.

And practically the same day a hundred years earlier, in 1867, Alfred Nobel patented an explosive made of nitroglycerin, sorbents and stabilizers, known as Nobel's Blasting Power or dynamite.

[]

It was predicted to be a beautiful spring day in Ohio. The rains had passed through earlier in the week and the temperature was almost hot for that time of year, in the upper sixties. The whole town was preparing to fete Bill Richards, who had just returned from Washington, D.C., where he was named one of four outstanding young farmers in the nation.[21] A parade was planned through town at six o'clock, followed by a reception at the St. Philip's Episcopal Church Parish House. Young people were getting ready for a dance at the Youth Canteen that night. The SHAGs, a popular local rock 'n' roll band, were going to play.[22] It was supposed to be a good day, a fun day. No one saw the dark cloud brewing over Holbrook's head.

Holbrook spent the early part of Saturday morning at Eshelman's Feed Mill, where he had worked for well over twenty years. The mill was across the street from his *former* home, where his wife still lived. "His fellow mill workers watched him busily nailing together a small wooden box. They said it was about fifteen inches by twelve inches by six inches. They didn't think to ask him what it would be," wrote Circleville resident, Harold Snook[23], in a personal memory of the disaster.

Arnold and his wife were at his mom's house that morning. "I don't think I was twenty-one yet," said Arnold. "I lived on Scioto Street at the time, on the other side of downtown. I had been married for maybe two years and my wife was *very* pregnant, like eight months pregnant at the time." Arnold, his wife and his mom had just returned from the Sertoma Club's Aunt Jemima Pancake Day breakfast held at the Grange that morning. When they got home, one of them noticed Holbrook's dirty brown Chevy parked across the street at the mill.

"We hadn't been there but a few minutes when, all of a sudden, we heard mom scream. We jumped up and ran into the kitchen to find my mom, dad and Uncle Sherman in a fight. My dad had a big knife of some kind, probably a butcher knife out of the kitchen drawer. He apparently had come to the house to threaten or kill my mother. My Uncle Sherman showed up out of nowhere and he stopped him. He fought him off. If my Uncle Sherman hadn't come by, my dad would have probably killed my mother right there. My dad ran out the back door and jumped into his old Chevy and fled off. 'You'll never work there again,' he yelled at my mom as he was leaving."

At 11:40 a.m. the Pickaway County Sherriff's office received a frantic call from someone in Holbrook's family reporting that Holbrook had beaten and cut his estranged wife at her home, according to a newspaper account. Minutes counted and yet time was lost because the call had to be re-routed to the City Police Department. City Patrolman Jack Mills was soon dispatched. When he finally arrived at the home, he took the report and learned that Holbrook was on his way uptown to Bingman's Drug Store.

"In all the excitement, someone called the cops," continued Arnold. "I don't know if it was my Uncle or my wife. And here they came, roaring up to the house with lights flashing. The policeman said, "Hop in the car," so my wife, eight months pregnant, my mother and I hopped into the cruiser and we roared downtown. The policeman roared downtown with red lights and siren blasting, my wife and I in the back, my mother in the front seat.

"All of a sudden, we heard and felt the blast; and the officer stopped the car on a dime, just like something out of the movies. And we stopped right under the stop light at downtown Court and Main. We must have gotten there thirty seconds after the bomb went off. Flames were leaping out of the building. People were screaming and running and yelling. The police officer jumped out of the cruiser and said, 'Lock the doors and don't move.' We were half a block from Bingman's. I had a grandstand seat and could see the whole thing. We must have missed the explosion by seconds."

Arnold seemed to have left the room for a moment as he remembered being in that car. His eyes were wide and his voice was full of dread.   This was the first time that Arnold remembered ever telling someone his story, that he was there on that day and had seen his dad for the last time driving off in a rage. This was the nugget of the story that lived inside of him for fifty years. He had held this memory so close to his chest that it seemed to have settled into his breathing.

Dynamite

"State arson investigators said the bomb contained twenty-five sticks of dynamite. It reportedly had been set off by a three-minute fuse." [24]

The official police and fire reports do not seem to exist. The only record of what happened I gleaned from newspaper articles and interviews. Yet, to my amazement, Chief Temple and Arnold Holbrook were able to tell me the same story, providing details that answered a question that had been on my mind for nearly fifty years: *How would someone even know how to make a bomb?*

When I was young, I speculated that Holbrook did his research in the public library. That was the only way I could figure that he could have learned how to do this. Yet, I knew that if I had tried something like that, the librarian would have called my mother to report my strange fascination with blowing things up; and my mother would have ended my fascination quickly all the way home and punctuated the lesson with a "switch" to my behind.

Chief Temple, however, knew a few things about dynamite and he didn't mind sharing. "Back then, many folks used dynamite. If you worked in the coal mines, you knew how to use it. Farmers used it sometimes to break up rocks or tree stumps," he said. "Hardware stores couldn't stock it in town, but if you needed some, you just told the owner and he would go to the shed he kept out on his farm and bring it in the next day.

"Dynamite was wrapped in oil paper. If it was wet, you needed to be careful because that was the glycerin weeping out. You lined up the sticks together and pinched the sticks at the top to get them to go off together. You used your teeth to bite the sticks together, to get a good pinch," said Chief Temple, pantomiming these actions. "You stuck the fuse in just right and it burned an inch a minute. If you wanted twenty minutes, you used twenty inches."

"I think I know where the dynamite came from," Arnold told me, and he talked in the same vein as the Chief. "I think it came from my grandfather's farm. I remember going to the barn as a kid and playing with the stuff. Horrors! I could have killed myself.

"Back then, farmers used dynamite to get rid of things that were in the way. If they had a big tree stump, they didn't bother digging it up or sawing it up. They bore a hole in the ground, put a stick of dynamite in and ran. It was over, it was done.

"In those days, you could go to a hardware store and buy a stick of dynamite. Just fork over the fifty cents or a dollar. They would sell the fuse on a roll, like a piece of wire, and whack it off and give it to you. You simply stuck it into the end of the dynamite and lit it. That was it. You bought a dynamite fuse by the minute. So many inches equal so many minutes. Just do the math. Snip it off and light it."

I was surprised that both men knew how to do this. Was this something guys learned in Boy Scouts or Industrial Arts class while the girls were in Home Ec? All the newspapers had reported that Holbrook had been a demolition expert in the military. And that had made sense. Arnold chuckled when he refuted that: "No, my father was not a demolition expert in the military." It was one of the details the papers got wrong that day.

Dynamite was used in coal mining because it was a "cool" explosive, unlikely to start a fire around coal dust. Would Holbrook have known that? Was Holbrook just trying to remove the building or the people inside, too? Whatever his intention, he probably didn't anticipate that the main gas line would rupture. Sort of the extra punch to the deed, as when the Twin Towers folded after the planes crashed into them on 9/11.

Three Minutes in Slow Motion

A witness later told (Patrolman Jack) Mills that Holbrook entered the store carrying the wooden box covered with a coat. As Holbrook walked by the lunch counter where his wife normally worked, a teenager (looked over and) remarked, "Hey mister, your box is smoking."" A woman employee who first saw him did not understand until Holbrook took her by the arm and said, "you better get out of here. I have a bomb."" (She was stunned and didn't move.) He was heard saying, "Don't try to stop me. I have a bomb and I mean business."[25]

There is a time gap between when Holbrook was seen raging at his wife and when he walked into Bingman's an hour later. Reports are that he went to the Eagles Lodge, drank and played cards with some buddies, and told them what he was going to do, that he was going to blow up Bingman's. Shouldn't these men have stepped up? But who would have believed the rant?

"At 12:48 p.m. Holbrook stopped outside Bingman's on the front sidewalk, lit a fuse sticking out of a wooden box, dropped his lighter on the sidewalk, and walked into the drug store."[26] As Holbrook walked into the store, the stock boy, Scott Lindsay, was up front in the store with pharmacist Bob Scranton, helping a customer look for hair product on a top shelf. Out of the corner of their eyes, both Scott and Bob saw Holbrook come into the store. Scott did not know Holbrook, other than that he was a customer. A few seconds later, though, both noticed by sight and smell that Holbrook was carrying something, a smoking box with a coat over it. They say "curiosity killed the cat," and it almost did when Scott innocently followed behind Holbrook trying to catch up with him to say something about his smoking package. (I can hear him say in his politest voice, "Hey Mister, your box is smoking…") Holbrook made it to the pharmacy, and as he was placing the box on the counter, Scott came up behind him and harmlessly reached for the package.

Holbrook reacted swiftly and, to Scott's shock, punched him and knocked him hard to the ground. Store owner Charlie Schieber was standing right there, behind the pharmacy counter, watching this altercation. Sensing danger, maybe having known about Holbrook's threats, Charlie snatched the package and ran around the corner and down the new hallway, toward the back door and the alley. Holbrook raced after Charlie and caught up with him halfway down the hall. Holbrook began punching Charlie with his fist, while Charlie hunkered over the "football." Pharmacist Ted Foster was in the prescription area behind the pharmacy counter and looked up in time to see the two men speed around the corner. Without hesitation, Ted took off after them, around the corner and down the hallway. Reaching the two in struggle, Ted fought with Holbrook to get him off his boss. Scott, stunned for a few seconds by Holbrook's punch, jumped up and ran after the men, toward the hall. Just as he was turning the corner, the bomb went off. The last thing Scott may have seen was Mart Lagore at the back door, clocking in for her shift.

The blast hurled Scott to the floor, hard on his back, and knocked him momentarily unconscious. When he came to, he thought maybe he was blind because he couldn't see a thing, but it was because of the thick black soot in the air. His glasses had been knocked off, so he felt around and found them. He jumped up and tried to get into the hallway where he had last seen his boss, but it was a disaster zone. In a fit of shock, adrenaline, and fear for his colleagues, Scott raced out the front door, jumping over debris in his way. He darted down the sidewalk, turned up the alley and headed to the back of the store. He tried to get into the building through the back door, but it was horribly jammed. That's where a first responder found him, realized that he was hurt, and rushed him immediately to the hospital. There, Scott was treated for "an abrasion to the forehead" and ruptured ear drums.[27]

[]

Joe Tomlinson was scheduled to work at Bingman's on Saturday from one to nine. His jobs that day were to put out stock in the afternoon and work the front register in the evening. New merchandise had arrived at the rear door and Joe's job was to either put it out on the floor or take it down to the basement for storage.

One of the perks of working at Bingman's was that employees could help themselves to food at the soda counter. Joe arrived a little early that day so he could get something to eat before he started his shift. He walked in the back door, said hello to Mrs. Willison in the office preparing payroll, and went straight to the soda fountain. As it was Saturday, the store was extremely busy, so instead of bothering the waitresses, he helped himself at the soda fountain. He was in the middle of fixing a milkshake when -- BOOM! -- the bomb went off. That was the last sound he would hear for several days.

The explosion knocked him to the floor and unconscious for a minute. Coming to, Joe was in shock and clueless as to what had just happened or the danger he was in. Almost laughable all these years later, Joe's immediate concern was for an expensive shipment of the men's popular after-shave, Jade East Cologne. It was in the basement waiting to be sent back to the manufacturer, a job he had been assigned that day. Worried that the shipment had been damaged, Joe jumped straight up, sprinted to the basement steps in the middle of the store and ran down to search for the prized boxes. Hearing nothing (because of the explosion) and seeing just a big mess and blinding black soot, he swiftly returned to the first floor. There, Joe looked around and saw no one else in the dark, soot-filled, bombed-out store. That was his last memory until someone found him a little while later, a few blocks away on Scioto Street, wandering in a daze.

Rescue

Those at the scene did as much as humanly possible to save persons in the store without the slightest delay or second thoughts to their own safety.[28]

Dennis Brown and City Patrolman Jack Mills were the first two people to reach the store. The newspapers reported that these first responders may have helped more than ten people out of the building. "These two men pulled people out of the building, stopped random cars on the street, and requisitioned private citizens to take the injured to the hospital," said Chief Temple, praising their spontaneous action. "A lot of people were inside. At first, no one knew how many people to look for." Witnesses estimated as many as thirty-five people might have been in the store when the blast went off.

Dennis Brown was the first on the scene. He was a junior at Circleville Bible College and worked across the street at J.C. Penney's. He had landed that job about six months before by pestering the store manager. The third time he went in to ask for a job, he looked around the store and saw clothing falling off hangers, merchandise a mess, and customers waiting in a long line. He marched up to Mr. Furman, the manager, and said, "Don't tell me you don't need help. Look around at this store, at the clothes on the floor, at the line." Furman was amused and hired him on the spot.

Dennis was from Lancaster, a town about thirty miles east of Circleville. His mom and dad worked at Circleville Bible College, which was a big reason why Dennis was a student there. His goal was to be a missionary, taking the word of God to far-off places. He would become a missionary soon enough, but not before his faith and mettle were tested that day.

At a few minutes before one, Dennis was about ten feet from the front door, ringing up a customer at the cash register. The entire front of J.C. Penney's was glass, floor to ceiling, windows and doors. Dennis remembered that he was staring straight out the front door at the exact time of the explosion. With eyes wide-open, Dennis watched as the front windows of Bingman's blew out, debris flying into the streets and hitting and cracking J.C. Penney's windows. Without hesitation or a moment to consider his safety, Dennis raced across the street and into the store.

"The fire didn't start immediately after the explosion, but, nonetheless, there was a lot of smoke coming out of the building," Dennis told me. When he entered the store, it was pitch black, dense with soot. People were lying everywhere, some only starting to move, others in shock, knocked out, blinded by flying glass, or in a state of confusion. Dennis was the first one into the store and from somewhere he heard, "There are people in the back." He ran to the back and was able to reach the pharmacy counter. He hopped over it, but he didn't get much further as the ceiling was beginning to cave in. The smoke was so bad, he couldn't see his own hands. His senses were on high alert, and he realized that he was in a dangerous spot. He scurried back over the counter and wasn't fifteen feet on the other side when the ceiling over the pharmacy area came crashing down. He gave up on getting to the back, and turned around to help people lying on the floor in front of him. Then he got himself out.

"Looking back, I was working on adrenaline and instinct. I didn't know the folks at Bingman's who died. I probably had seen them, but I didn't know them."

Newspaper accounts described the mayhem in the store after the explosion. "Those who did not realize the situation did not have time to take cover. Others who saw everything were glued to the spot. No one had time to dash for the door.

"Initial reports indicated at least seven or more persons were missing. A small child, presumed missing at first, later turned up at her grandmother's house with a bruise on her head.[29]

Fighting the Fire

A two-inch gas main ran down the back alley. The explosion from the bomb cut the gas line in two. "Flames were coming out of the gas line like a Bunsen burner." – Chief Temple

The blast that rocked the town could be felt two miles away. The Circleville fire station was only a few blocks away, so firefighters were on the scene within minutes. The fire should have been contained quickly, but a two-inch gas main at the rear of the building was severed by the blast and it took firefighters over an hour to shut it off. Driven by strong westerly winds, the fire quickly and unexpectedly whipped into a frenzy, consuming two adjacent buildings to the west and threatening to jump the alley and take out the whole block.

Bystanders jumped into action, "some battling the blaze in soaked dress suits, others in Bermuda shorts. News of the explosion and fire went out on the air waves. Off-duty firemen and firemen from neighboring communities rushed into town to join in the battle. Town folk helped with hoses, and carried sandwiches and water to firemen. The Mayor passed out soft drinks to the weary workers. City councilmen manned brooms to keep the street clear from glass. Lindsey's Bake Shop sent trays of doughnuts and baked goods of all kinds to firefighters and rescuers who could not take time out."[30]

The fire burned hot. The heat grew so intense it melted signs on nearby buildings and kept firefighters at a distance. Circleville had just purchased a new ladder truck that was damaged during the blaze, all of the rear plastic coverings having melted off.

A dense cloud of smoke, visible fifteen miles away, engulfed the downtown area and added to the confusion in the streets. Police tried to take control of the scene, but folks had flocked downtown and there was mayhem. People were milling about, many in a state of shock, horrified by the scene: flames shooting out of three buildings. The streets were littered with debris from the blast and filled with merchandise from store owners evacuating their neighboring buildings, fearful of the raging and uncontrolled fire. "Onlookers winced as the city's policemen used their pistols to shoot out safety glass windows in upper floor apartments to allow water to be poured on the blaze."[31] A power failure caused by the blast created additional problems for center city merchants and rescue workers for nearly two hours. The local newspaper was about halfway through its regular press run at the time. A second Saturday edition reporting the bombing and fire came off the presses about four in the afternoon, after electricity was restored.[32]

It took two grueling hours to bring the fire under control. "The bomb hit with devastating force. Workers found a five-foot diameter hole in the wooden floor with a pit two feet deep filled with a mix of charred wood and soil, apparently left by the explosion. The blast put a hole in the east wall of the store next to Wardell's Carpet and Rug store... The blast blew out windows of the drug store and broke windows in other stores across Main Street."[33] The Circleville Water Department reported that nearly one and a half million gallons of water had been pumped.[34] "Cleaning up, City Policeman Richard Blaney found a lighter which is believed to have been the one Holbrook used to ignite the bomb before he entered the store."[35]

Chief Temple talked to me about the investigation. "At the time, we didn't know if Holbrook had been killed or if he was still on the loose. The police went to Holbrook's apartment at the Danny Lee Motel, but people were saying that the police were overstepping their authority, that they should get a search warrant before they entered his room." An officer called Temple in exasperation, and Temple told him "go into Gourmet Corner and get a witness to go with you to enter the apartment." The police, with their witness in tow, forced the door in and found the remaining dynamite, caps and fuses. The newspaper reported, "A writing pad, found in the motel where Holbrook was staying was scrutinized by city police and members of the London [Ohio] Investigation Bureau. Written on it were 'fifty sticks of dynamite for Bingman's Drugs.' The handwriting, yet to be proven as Holbrook's, is still under investigation."[36]

But for the Grace of God

On that lovely Saturday morning, my mom had arranged to pick up three of our former neighbor's kids to hang out with us for the day. Our station wagon had that magical third, rear-facing seat that allowed my mom to stuff eight kids into place.

Ken and Lois Osborn had children similarly aged to my siblings and me. They had recently move into town, but we had kept our friendship strong on the memories of rampaging together through the back yards of Knollwood Village.

My ten-year-old brother, my twelve-year-old sister and the two similarly-aged Osborn kids wanted to go bowling. My mom dropped them off downtown, and the kids had a tussle about where they would go first, to the bowling alley or Bingman's. The bowling alley won. My mom had arranged to pick them up at Bingman's later, after the rest of us went grocery shopping. My dad was working that day, and Bingman's soda fountain and magazine rack would entertain them until mom could get there.

My two younger brothers, who were three and five at the time, my "twin" Osborn, Janet, and I tagged along with my mom to the grocery store. Back then, we shopped on the north side of town, at the Super Duper.

About an hour later, with shopping completed, we were driving toward home on North Court Street when we felt the muffled blast. As we got closer to town, about the time we reached our turnoff to go home, we saw black smoke billowing from downtown. My mom's first words were, "Let's go find out what's going on." But as we got closer, her voice turned to dread, saying, "That's Bingman's Drugs. That's Bingman's Drugs!" My mom turned on the radio to find the local news, because in that era every town had a radio station that kept us all up to date, like an audio Outlook Calendar and Facebook page rolled into one. It took us less than five minutes to get downtown, and the streets were a mess, some blocked off. My mom was driving madly at this point and got within half a block of the drug store, maneuvering our station wagon through back streets and alleys. She was ultimately stopped when a guy literally jumped on the hood of her car and screamed, "Lady, you can't go any farther. It's not safe." My mom was forced to park the car and search on foot, and that's how a car full of kids came to be parked behind the bank at the corner of Court and Main. "Joni, fix a sandwich for your brothers and I'll be back," she said as she raced off, trying not to show her terror.

The bowling alley was in the basement of a building located a block up Main Street, on the other side of Court and Main. My older brother and sister and their Osborn friends had just finished bowling when the lights went out, leaving the bowling alley completely dark. Someone yelled that Bingman's was on fire, and the four of them -- Ty, Tom, Karen and Karen Osborn -- dashed out in panic into the daylight of Main Street.

My sister's account is slightly different than Karen Osborn's account of what happened next. As my sister told me, "Karen and I got to Court and Main and the place was full of people, the road cordoned off and a thick crowd had gathered, reminding me of the Pumpkin Show (where the town shuts down for a week of carnivals, food trucks and parades)." In this case, though, the crowd was milling about watching flames lap out of buildings half a block away. It was too much mayhem and confusion for my sister. Her memory is that she and her friend Karen turned around and walked back to the Osborn's house about a mile away.

Karen Osborn's version had them in the chaos for much longer. "The fire seemed like it was right on top of us even though we were half a block away. The fire was enormous and raging out of control. The commotion on the street was chaotic, with firemen frantic and disorganized in the chaos. We ran down the street into the crowd and it was frightening, overwhelming because we got separated from each other for a while." My brother, Ty, who was only ten at the time, and Tom Osborn, who might have been eleven, took off into the crowd.

Mrs. Osborn was at home when she heard the news about Bingman's. With the terrifying thought that her kids could be in that fire, she ran out of the house, jumped in the car and raced the mile into downtown to find them. She may have been with her husband, too, because both ended up being downtown immediately. Who knows how long it took, but the determined mother found her kids, Karen and Tom, and my sister, and took them back to her home.

My brother, Ty, though, was separated from the rest. His memory is that he stood in the crowd for a long time, staring at the burning buildings completely convinced that his dad had gotten out, even though the stories were jumping from person to person that Ted and Charlie were last seen fighting with Holbrook when the box exploded. I was told years later by my mom that Ty was found wandering around the alley behind Bingman's, looking for his dad. Ty just remembers saying to himself that he was sure dad had gotten out. *Of course, he got out.* I always pictured Ty at the back door of Bingman's walking about in a daze and maybe tears of shock. As I know now, though, he wouldn't have been able to get that close, as the gas line that was fueling the fire was in the back alley. Neither of us knows who found him or how he got home that day.

It's also a mystery to me how Mr. Osborn found our station wagon parked behind the bank. I just remember Mr. Osborn's smiling, calm face as it popped into view through the car window. He had the keys to my mom's car and he whisked us off to his house where we continued playing upstairs. We knew something had happened but nothing was explained to us. We were kids after all. The adults hadn't had time to figure out what it all meant, much less how to explain what was happening to their children. Karen Osborn and I both have a sketchy memory of that day, of both our families -- minus my father -- gathered in the Osborn's family room, all sitting there in a daze and in shock.

Another friend of the family, Earl Palm, found my mom in the midst of the mayhem. Earl was a bear of a man, figuratively as well as physically; a smiling, kind and gentle bear. He was both a farmer and a banker; a success in one (eventually becoming the president of the bank) and a hobbyist in the other (a weekend, gentleman farmer). He and his family had been in Circleville for many generations and were -- and are -- pillars in the community. Even today, long retired, he could be found most mornings having coffee at the usual spot and yapping it up with fellow retired "townies" in Circleville.

Earl Palm had five kids. My dad had five kids. Seems only right that they would become friends, and their wives would become friends, and their kids would become friends.

The Palms lived on a farm nestled behind the fairgrounds on the edge of town. To get to their house, you went down a lane, across a rickety bridge and up the hill. They had a new house built next to the old farmhouse, a ramshackle building with surprising nooks and crannies that we kids explored many a day. Looking across the field in front of the house, I could still imagine seeing all the kids together on hay rides behind a tractor driven by Earl. I can still hear the laughter as we held on tightly, trying not to fall off the bales that sat on the rickety flatbed trailer.

"Your mother was a strong lady, before the accident and afterward," Earl's wife, Jeannie, said. "I remember going to a dance at the Grange and then going over to your parent's house afterward. Both Earl and Ted had too much to drink. I had Earl, and Eileen had Ted, walking them up and down the street to sober them up," she said, chuckling. And Earl added, with a warm smile, "I can show you the claw marks on my ear(lobe) from where your mom pulled us to her will."

Earl was at work that day. The bank had recently moved to East Main Street, near the bowling alley. "We felt the explosion and I went down the street to find out what happened. I remember that day because my dad, Russell, was in the habit of taking my kids downtown on Saturdays to Bingman's for a malt. They were downtown that day, but I don't know why they weren't in there except that divine powers had kept them away."

The whole town was standing around watching the firemen fighting to put out the blaze. "We were all in shock. People on the street were talking, piecing together what happened." Earl discovered my mom in the middle of that turmoil.

I can only imagine the horror for my mom, yet I have only heard reports about how calm she was. She watched the fire amid the mayhem for a while. Then, when she was entirely convinced that her husband was in fact gone and her children were safe, she turned to Earl and asked him to take her to the church, the First Methodist Church.[37] Earl recalled entering the sanctuary with her, and said my mom walked right up to the altar rail, knelt down and prayed. He timidly joined her at the rail. My mom wasn't a Holy Roller but she had the old-time faith that God was the answer. Put your troubles in the hands of God. "Come unto me, all ye that labor and are heavy laden, and I will give you rest."[38] She was also in deep shock. Later, Earl took my mom home and was by her side "to tell you kids that you no longer had a father."

Heard It on the Radio

The night before that fateful Saturday, Francis and Chuck Willison bought a half-dozen rose bushes. Before going to work the next morning, Francis and Chuck were outside, Chuck with a shovel and Francis offering directions, saying, "How about one here and one there…?"

Jim, their middle child, was eight at the time. His brother, Rick, was eleven; and the youngest son, Gary, was seven, in first grade. I interviewed Jim and his father in separate conversations, and the following narrative intertwines their memories of the day.

"Surprisingly, I remember a lot about that day, and I don't know why," Jim started. "I can't tell you anything about the day before or the day after, or two years before or two years after, but I can tell you about that day. I don't have many memories of my mom, but as for that day, I remember.

"My mom and dad were planting rose bushes that day. We had only been in the house a few years, not very long, and they were doing a little landscaping around the house. It was a warm Saturday. We were cutting the grass. My older brother was eleven and we had a riding mower, and I can't remember if he was on the riding mower or the push mower, but I remember Mom saying, 'I wish he wouldn't do that.' She didn't think he was old enough. And then she left. I remember where her car was parked."

About midmorning, Francis went to work. Chuck spent the rest of the afternoon finishing the work, digging holes and planting the roses. "Saturdays for us were *putzing* around the house and doing yardwork," Jim continued. "I remember, after my mom left, a little while later, standing along the tree line between our house and the neighbor's house, where our cousin lived. We were standing there and dad looked up and said, 'There's a bunch of smoke coming from town.' We looked due west, and there was a big plume of smoke. If I could draw, I would draw you a picture of what it looked like. And we said, 'Yeah, looks like somebody set something on fire in town.' We lived in a wooded area and it was common for us to set stuff on fire, shrubs, extra limbs. For us, it didn't seem a big deal at all."

A little while later, Chuck went into the kitchen and turned on the radio. That's how he heard about the explosion at Bingman's Drug Store.

Jim remembered a few more details. "It was later that day, still in the afternoon, I was still outside with my younger brother Gary. Suddenly, Dad came tearing out and said, 'Get in the car!' It wasn't one of these 'Get in the car,' like 'Go get your jacket." It was 'GET IN THE CAR AND LET'S GO!!' And, so, we drove to town. He apparently had seen something on TV or the radio. At the time, I didn't know what was happening."

"I loaded up the kids in the car," said Chuck. "My mother and dad had retired and had a house on East Franklin Street." He remembers dropping off the kids at his parent's house, and then driving up and parking in the lot behind J.C. Penney's. Chuck went through the alley to Main Street, coming out on the other side of the street right in front of Bingman's. By the time that he got there, the fire was out and firefighters were in the building. "Having worked at Wardell's and downtown for so long, I knew some of the cops and firemen and city police. I started across the street and a policeman or fireman grabbed ahold of me and told me, 'You aren't going in there.'"

Francis almost always worked on Saturdays. It was payday for the Bingman's employees and she had a role in that. Charlie wrote the checks and gave them out. Employees would take the check straight back to the office, sign it over to the store, and Francis would give them cash. Her ritual every Saturday, first thing, was to go to the bank and get enough cash to have on hand for this exchange. Chuck thought, "Either Francis was in there or, I was hoping, Francis had gone to the bank and hadn't gotten back yet."

Chuck's memory of the day ended here.

Jim remembers some details slightly differently. "We parked not in our usual place, but we parked, and Dad said, 'Stay in the car!' It wasn't a request, it was 'STAY IN THE CAR!' There was a lot of activity around us. We didn't know why we were there, but we never left the car. We were probably in the car an hour when my granddad came down and got the car and drove us back to his house.

"Grandma and Grandpa weren't in good health and so it wasn't necessarily fun to go to their house. It was a place we went regularly, but it wasn't entertainment. We were at Grandma's house, and at some point, somebody told us, I don't remember who, 'There was an explosion downtown at the place where your mom works and we are trying to find her.'

"I remember sitting on the couch, listening to my grandma's radio. We were listening to the local radio station, 107.1 FM. The radio was up on her mantel, above a fireplace that hadn't been used in fifty years. I don't believe the radio was normally there, because I don't remember ever seeing it again in that place. Of course, the local radio station was a lifeline. That was how we knew what was going on. I don't think that's what sparked my interest in commercial broadcasting later in life, but it probably had something to do with it, knowing full well that people like me, everybody, was listening to the radio. It was the only thing we could do. I don't remember eating, I don't remember drinking, I don't remember going to the bathroom. I remember sitting on that couch knowing that things had changed, yet not really understanding the gravity of what had changed.

"Years later, starting when I was sixteen, I worked at the same radio station. WNRE, named after the owner, Nelson Robert Embrey. We always called it affectionately, 'With No Real Effort,'" Jim chuckled, remembering good times.

"By the time that I had hired on, the studios and transmitters were located out on Route 23. But I had the opportunity to go downtown during one of the Pumpkin Shows because we broadcasted the parades from the second floor of the old studio. I went upstairs and it was a 'Twilight Zone' moment, if you will. I remember going up the stairs thinking the whole time, *This is where they were talking when I was listening to the radio when I was eight.* I made a point of walking down the hall. It was just a small hall and, on the right, was the studio. I walked into the studio. When I was in that studio, in my mind, I was eight years old again, sitting on my grandma's couch. And I remembered thinking, *The microphone is gone, but that's the same microphone boom they used to broadcast that day.* I was eight years old in my mind, and pictured them talking in this very room about my mom and about the incident. It was a poignant moment."

Coming back to his memories of that day, Jim continued: "There were lots of people going in and out of Grandma's house that day. My mom's sister and her husband, Mildred and George Schmidt, came in. And I knew they shouldn't have been there. They didn't know where my dad's mom lived. Seeing them walk in, and Mildred walked in first -- which I would expect, because it was her sister -- I knew it was bad. It's one of those things, when I saw them, I knew I wasn't going to see mom that night.

"It was daylight when we got to Grandma's house. It was well past dark when we left. Mildred and George drove us home. We didn't see my dad until the next morning. Gary and I shared a room, and we went to bed. Gary and I whispered under the sheets until we fell asleep, 'Well, this might have happened,' or 'Mom might be over there,' or 'Let's get out and find out what's going on.'

"I'm sure we got up early; we were farm boys, worked early shifts and things like that. We got up, and Dad said, 'Come on back, boys. We need to talk,' and he told us."

Jim's strong radio voice waivered for just a second, and then he was quiet for a time.

Bystanders' Stories

"News got out on the AP that the center of town had been annihilated by a bomb, and the phone lines were jammed with people calling to see about their loved ones. We had to quickly get a new story out on the AP in order to get the phones working again. But there came a point when we had to evacuate some of the streets down Pinckney and up Main. My mother lived on West Main Street and my wife called her to tell her to leave. She said she had heard something, but she wasn't leaving because she had a cake in the oven." – Chief Bob Temple

Honestly, when I started writing this story, I thought the story was about me and my family, and maybe about the others who lost loved ones in the event. Yet strangers and friends kept popping up, talking about the event from their perspective -- where they were at the time, what they were doing, how it affected them -- tiny slivers of the story. "I should have been there that morning." "I was on my way." "I had just left." "I fought the fire." "I heard the blast." "I knew someone in there." "I thought my kids were there, my husband, my mother, my friend." "I was so scared." "I lived a few blocks away."

At first, I thought these people were completely insensitive, trying to *steal* the story from us. I wasn't alone thinking that way. Charlie Schieber's son Larry, who also became a pharmacist and store owner in Circleville, expressed similar feelings. "Sometimes people come up to me in my store and tell me what they were doing that day. They were on their way to the store or they had just left. It can seem a little insensitive to hear their stories. The story had such a dramatic impact on our lives," said Larry.

Joe Tomlinson shared a similar view. "Sometimes I'm asked to retell the story at parties and friendly gatherings. I don't like to tell it, but I do. I feel like these strangers to the story don't understand the impact it had on me. It is a sacred story that they make into momentary entertainment."

Yet, I have come to realize that the blast sent ripples into the community, that bystanders and survivors are a part of this story, too. For instance, Mart Lagore's niece told me sadly that Mart wasn't scheduled to work that day, but one of the other ladies had called in sick. She remembered this well because for years afterward, that lady continually apologized to the family for being sick that day.

From newspaper accounts, I learned some of the survivors' tales:

Mr. and Mrs. Wardell were in the carpet store next door. Mrs. Wardell was standing near the front window. She was knocked down during the explosion and the window was blown out. Mr. Wardell was in the back, sorting out a new shipment of rugs. The pile of rugs was tall enough to catch the ceiling beam as it fell, and thick enough to save Mr. Wardell from the blast, whose epicenter was less than ten feet and two brick walls from where he was standing.

Mary Crable, mother of two grown children, was a waitress at the store's lunch counter. She was standing behind the soda fountain, not paying much attention "because the counter was full." The next thing she remembered was being knocked to the floor by the explosion. Unhurt, she helped a shaken female customer from the store. She recalled the dazed customer commenting, "I'll have to pay my bill later."[39]

Three sixteen-year-old Circleville High School sophomores were lunching at Bingman's after a morning's hard work on a Service Over Self Club project. They changed seats because they smelled fumes from the bomb. A second later, the blast hurled them off their stools and on top of each other. They made their way out of the store through the black smoke and piles of debris. One of the teenagers described the sound of the blast as "just unimaginable."[40]

The Mayor passed by the drug store about five minutes before the explosion. "I normally eat in the drugstore on Saturdays, but I decided to eat at the Mecca (a nearby restaurant) because I had to do some shopping today," he said. [41]

Mr. and Mrs. Fred Wickerham lived with their son and daughter in the apartment over the drugstore. The couple and their daughter were at the fairgrounds at the time of the blast. Their teenage son, Nick, was in the apartment and escaped unhurt. All of the family's possessions were destroyed.[42]

Beverly Strassel, twenty-three, lived in an apartment over a realty company adjacent to the buildings that burned. Her four-year-old son had been playing near the disaster area minutes before the blast. "He came in just in time," she told the newspaper, sobbing. She was treated for shock at Berger Hospital.

News traveled fast and far. George Iles, in the service in Saigon, turned on his radio at six a.m. and heard about the explosion in Circleville. In Saigon they were accustomed to bombings, but he found it unbelievable that such a thing could happen in Circleville.[43]

Newspaper commentary added feeling to the day with these observations:

Most everything stopped when people learned of the fire. Businesses closed, housewives stopped what they were doing, and everyone who wasn't actively helping seemed suspended in time. The fire was uppermost in the minds of all. Tasks that couldn't wait were done automatically and people didn't even remember having done them. Even after the fire was brought under control and the number of dead was known, the feeling of eeriness did not leave. Everyone except the workers talked quietly -- even they only raised their voices when necessary. The awesomeness was not felt by many until Monday morning when they attempted to resume their daily routine. It seemed to many that the air was heavy and our minds did not respond quickly.[44]

Hospital

"We filled the hospitals. Doctors and nurses came in droves." — *Chief Temple*

"Phyllis Holbrook later appeared about midafternoon at Berger Hospital in a state of shock after she learned of the actions of her husband. She was placed under sedation and kept overnight for observation."[45]

Tiny Berger Hospital, only a mile from downtown, went quickly into high alert. Eight off-duty doctors and more than thirty nurses were called in, some instinctively dropping everything and running to help after feeling the blast and seeing the smoke billowing from downtown. The injured arrived in waves, delivered by strangers who had been conscripted by first responders on Main Street and directed to take the wounded to the hospital.

For a time, those who had heard the inaccurate Associated Press report describing the whole town as decimated called the hospital looking for loved ones. The hospital switchboard was overwhelmed with frantic calls from mothers searching for their kids who might have been at Bingman's. Town folk flooded the emergency room entrance looking for information and reassurance.

Twenty-four people in all were treated for injuries, mostly from the blast; surprisingly, none was seriously hurt. A first responder, William Goff, thirty-one and a former Circleville policeman, was injured when a metal extension ladder toppled and struck him. Goff had joined in the firefighting when he saw smoke and ran to help. He realized he couldn't get in the building, so he picked up a fire hose and began spraying water into the buildings. He had worked about forty-five minutes when the ladder fell. He was transported to Berger Hospital with a broken right leg. "There wasn't any hope..." Goff said from his hospital bed a couple of hours later.[46]

"Mrs. Leona Stonerock was treated for shock caused from worry over a daughter not accounted for." [47] Mrs. Stonerock was Mart Lagore's mom.

Hospital patients listened to the news of the fire on radios, except one – Jean Schieber – wife of druggist and store owner Charlie Schieber. She had undergone minor surgery the day before. "The task of informing her of the tragedy was difficult almost beyond words, authorities said."

[]

"What happened after he did it?" Arnold began again, starting with a big sigh. "Oh man, everything was turned upside down. We were sitting in a police car at downtown Court and Main. It's coming back to me now. In the scuffle, in the kitchen when my father tried to kill mom, my very pregnant wife got right in the middle of it, and my dad knocked her down on the floor. She landed directly on her stomach."

I can't help but gasp.

"Oh, yes," Arnold continued. "And she was scared. And so was I. And she says, 'I might lose the baby.' And I thought, 'Oh my God, I hope not.' So, from Court and Main, the cop came back to the car and I said, 'Look, I've got to get my wife to the hospital.' And off he roars. He roars up to the emergency room," Arnold began talking more slowly, with longer pauses between sentences. "And I jumped out to help my wife. And she was crying and screaming. She was in a lot of pain. She thought she was going to lose the baby.

"I walked into the hospital, into a nightmare. All those people in the hospital, it was horrible." Arnold gave another big sigh and cleared his voice as he started to choke up. "People were sitting on the floor. They had them lying on the floor. There was blood everywhere. An older man was sitting in a chair and he had a big towel over his face, and the blood was dripping out of the towel, and the man was screaming." Arnold started talking faster, without pauses, in an agitated way as he remembered the scene. "And I thought, 'Oh God, I hope nobody recognizes me.' And some little kid comes up, I can't remember his name. He was a kid who worked at the drugstore. God, I wish I remembered his name. It was an afterschool job. He did odd jobs. And I walked around seeing all these people and this scrawny kid walked over and stared at me. His face was all black and half his hair was gone, and he said to me, "'It was your dad, Arnie.'

"I knew a lot of the people, over the years. I have forgotten half their names. But back then, I knew every one of them at Bingman's. It was like a big, happy family. I think Mom was the youngest one that worked there. She had worked there for ten years, as near as I can remember. Everybody practically came with the building."

And with that, Arnold needed a break.

Recovery

The explosion and fire of tremendous proportion that followed claimed at least five lives, destroyed three downtown businesses, and numerous upper level apartments and left the community grief-stricken... Buildings destroyed were Bingman's Drugs, Wardell Carpet and Rugs, and King's Department Store.[48]

"Fire Chief Bernard Wolfe said several sticks of dynamite were found in the rubble, unexploded."[49]

As the fire raged, workers from the local Dupont chemical plant brought in fire suits, "but we weren't going to go in when the fire was burning," Chief Temple said. "Finally, the fire was mainly out, and we got on the roof (with the ladder truck). There were still hot spots, but we started looking around and that's when we found your dad."

Chief Temple explained: "We staged at Mader's (Funeral Home) garage and laid the body parts out like a jigsaw puzzle." By Saturday evening, they had at least three positive identifications, even though some of the clues were only rings or dental work. It took until Sunday to confirm Charlie Schieber, having found his singed wallet still in his pants, with singed money inside. As bystanders looked on, firefighters under spotlights searched the ruins into the night for as many body parts as they could find, then returned in the morning to continue the search.

Jack Mader remembered helping his dad with the recovery efforts. He recalled that townsfolk were standing around watching. Many were right up inside of Bingman's and wouldn't move back a safe distance as the police tried to clear the area. Jack remembered one of the firemen, in exasperation, turning a firehose on the crowd to get them to move back.

Dean Gullick, barely a teenager at the time, remembered watching the recovery efforts. Three firemen, pulling aside debris in the hole made by the explosion, uncovered a body. They were so disturbed by the sight, they turned their heads in unison, and vomited.

By midday Sunday, they had most of the body parts they would find, but still had not made a positive identification of Holbrook. Chief Temple said sadly, "His kid came to the police station and asked me, 'Bob, have you found my dad yet?' and I told him, 'No, I'll call you.'"

Not finding Holbrook was also disconcerting to Chief Temple because, without a positive identification, he had to continue with an assumption that Holbrook could still be on the loose and planning additional actions. The chief put a police detail on the family, another at the Danny Lee Motel and a third detail on a man who also might have been the focus of Holbrook's rage. There was no proof, but enough concern to offer this protection.

Chief Temple had another issue, as well: "We had a problem trying to keep people out of the rubble, looters and people just curious. We had a problem because of all the drugs in there. We called the agency in Columbus responsible for the drugs and they told us that as long as we had the records of what was there, and we did, that we should go in there and smash every bottle we saw. And we did that. We went back in on the third day and did it again, and that's when we found a body part that didn't belong to Ted or Charlie."

Chief Temple continued: "On Tuesday, we called in Bob Baby[50] from Columbus, a really smart guy, to help us with the identification. He asked if we had checked with any medical records. And that's how we ended up at the hospital. We found that Holbrook had broken his hip on the job a while back, and the hospital had the X-rays. We took the torso that we found, X-rayed the hip, and compared it with the one on file. The bone breaks lined up and we knew, then, that we had Holbrook."

There was a rumor of a suicide note that Holbrook had mailed to his boss, the general manager at Eshelman's Mill. But the general manager hadn't turned the letter over to the police. Chief Temple was starting the process to get a court order for the letter, when they confirmed the body parts as belonging to Holbrook. After that, Temple let the rest of the investigation drop. They never recovered a suicide letter. Chief Temple explained to me, and gestured at the same time, "You wouldn't want to take a thorn out of one hand and then turn around and jab it into the other hand."

Chief Temple was visibly upset at a few points telling his story. He said he was tough as nails back then, but never had he seen anything so bad, even in the war. I worried during this interview that Chief Temple's version might have been too graphic for me. I had been hellbent on gathering as much exhaustive detail as I could find. Yet now, I might never clear this picture from my mind.

Goodbyes

Bingman's Drug Store was such a warm, friendly place. It will be greatly missed by the community.[51]

Four days later we were burying our beloveds. The Methodist Church hosted a double funeral for Charlie Schieber and my father, both steadfast members, on Wednesday at 10:30 a.m. Standing up for Charlie Schieber were his parents, wife and two children, ages seven and ten. Standing up for my dad were his mother (my grandmother), my mom and us five kids, spanning the ages of three to twelve.

The church was packed. The retractable wall that only disappeared at Easter and Christmas candlelight service was gone on that day, and the parlor was overflowing with townspeople and mourners. The paper reported in more detail:

> *Many stores closed their doors so employees could pay their last respects to the two men. American flags were raised throughout the city as a final tribute. The funeral procession followed a special route through the*

downtown section as a final tribute to two men who had been a part of the local business scene for numerous years. The Foresman Chimes were played in salute. Both Mr. Schieber and Mr. Foster were veterans. The flag observance was handled by the local America Legion Post.[52]

The send-off was immense because, as the newspaper pointed out, "Police and other observers have no doubt Mr. Schieber and Mr. Foster were the true heroes of Saturday's calamity… Their effort to dispose of the bomb … by way of a rear exit was fatal. … Many feel they could have reached the front door in time … but the death toll probably would have been greater if the explosive device had been tossed onto Main Street."[53]

Fifty years later, I was surprised by the newspaper account, to realize what a big deal the town made for the two men -- they were celebrated as heroes -- yet, the two women who lost their lives were laid to rest without public fanfare. As it was reported: "Mrs. Lawrence (Martha) Lagore, forty-five, was buried on Tuesday at 10:30 a.m. at the First EUB Church. She was survived by her husband, two adult children and her parents. Mrs. Charles (Francis) Willison, thirty-six, was eulogized on Wednesday at 2:30 p.m. at the funeral home. She was survived by her husband and three children."[54]

After the funeral, Charlie Schieber's remains were laid to rest in Bucyrus, in his native Crawford County. My dad and Mart Lagore were buried in Circleville's Forest Cemetery, their graves located near each other. My dad was buried underneath the canopy of an oak tree; the location marked by a simple, white marble military stone. Mart's husband and family honored her with a grand and lavish headstone. For years afterward, every time I visited the cemetery, I always noticed fresh flowers on her grave.

The paper reported that a private funeral and burial service were held for Holbrook on Thursday of that week. Holbrook, forty-three, was survived by his father, his wife, three children, one brother and two sisters.

The Circleville Area Chamber of Commerce set up a memorial fund, and the donations were eventually bequeathed to Berger Hospital to furnish a patient room. A memorial plaque still hangs on the entrance to what was then Room 119, dedicated to the memory of the four victims.

Jean Schieber received more than five hundred letters of condolence and support from the community, which she kept and passed down to her daughter, Karen, along with a scrapbook of memories and the singed and charred wallet of her father.

For many years afterward, on the anniversary of her death, Mart Lagore's family published a special tribute to her in the local paper's *In Memoriam* section at the beginning of the Classifieds. Here is one of the many poems I found:

> *The month of April again is here*
> *To us the saddest of the year.*
> *A bitter grief, a shock severe,*
> *To part with one we loved so dear.*
> *God gave us strength to face it,*
> *And courage to bear the blow,*
> *But what it meant to lose you,*
> *No one will ever know.*

Sadly, missed by Mother, Father, Sister, Niece and Nephew[55]

STORIES OF THE PEOPLE WHO LIVED ON

Butterflies and Shock Waves

A scientific theory of Chaos posits that little things can create unsuspectingly big impacts. The metaphor is "when a butterfly flaps its wings in Japan, America has a hurricane." If a butterfly can do that, just think about the energy of a bomb blast.

I thought about the event and its impact on our collective lives. I pictured three distinct patterns of waves. The first wave, like ripples when a stone is dropped in water, carried the immediate damage. The inner ring of people, those closest to the epicenter of the blast, felt the damage to their bodies. The victims' families felt the blast rip squarely through their hearts. The ripples undulated out to the first responders, the people who cleaned up, with graphic images permanently etched into their memories. Ripples moved outward, touching the good people who helped the victims' families adjust to the new day, making them kinder people and a bit more grateful for what they didn't lose. The outer ring of movement, softer, but still present for the on-lookers and bystanders, many of whom may have returned to their normal business even before the fire was out. Yet, even they were lifted ever so gently by an unsettled feeling that things would be different for a while.

The second wave of impact crashed into people's lives the next day, the next week, the next few years. How would their lives change? What new opportunities would open or close because five people were no longer available to play their unique roles in the world? Would the world be breathtakingly different? Would life be even better? Could things get worse? Would we even be able to recognize what changed?

The third wave would be accounted for years later, perhaps fifty years later, as the effects fell across time, the event still influencing the way we think and feel and love. Those would be the more subtler waves of insight; the "would haves," "could haves," and "should haves" that only roll in from distance and reflection. Out of the perspective of the third wave came the stories of looking back, of how people managed, how they eventually moved forward.

The after-stories changed in another way, too. Up until now, the stories were mainly about the men of the times. The pharmacists, the bomber, the first responders, all men. The women were bystanders, bit players in a drama that required action, strength, and bravery. Women didn't get on the ladders, or rush into the building, or lead the recovery efforts. Women didn't make the bomb. They were in the background, extras on the "set." This was the reality of women in the 1960s, the box they moved around in. Yet, afterward, women played a significant role in picking up the pieces. Thank goodness, then, when it was our time to stand up, society offered us a bit more room to maneuver.

Phyllis

"Circleville's grapevine is so strong, Tarzan could swing off it." –
A friend of my mom's

I have always been confused about a prominent story in the
Bible. King David had an affair with Bathsheba. When she got
pregnant, David ordered her husband, Uriah, into his death battle
so that the knowledge of his secret affair would not be revealed.
The chapter ends with, "But the thing David had done displeased
the Lord."[56] Knowing that David went on to become the greatest
king in history, I took this last line to mean that the Lord had a
moment of sadness but moved on. My lesson was that God
turned his head when boys acted out.

A man didn't want his wife working at the pharmacy so he
took a bomb in and blew the place up. It was such a casual
statement that, at nine years old, I took it as a logical thing to do.

No one stood up and said explicitly, 'That was wrong, that shouldn't have happened.' I mixed up the story of King David with a side story of this event: that a despondent man thought his wife was having an affair. That story became the underlying justification, and gave the husband a reason; it somehow shifted the weight of the blame onto the wife.

Phyllis Holbrook was hospitalized immediately after the event for shock and grief over what her husband had done. Now, consider what she had gone through for many years. Her son reported that, many times, her drunken husband beat her and threatened her life. Finding a community of co-workers at Bingman's, who lovingly had taken her under their care and concern, she found the courage to separate from her abusive partner. She filed for divorce just one month prior, using a judicial system that made divorce difficult and public. Her own life had been threatened that very day, her husband wielding a butcher knife intending to kill her that morning. However, the twist of the proverbial knife that killed her soul were the stories and rumors afterward that put the blame on her: Everyone believed that she was having an affair. The undercurrent almost seemed to justify Holbrook's actions. "Despondent husband." "Recently separated." There was no mention of his prior injustices and domestic brutality.

The newspaper tried to quash the rumors, saying, "Many stories are circulating as to why Holbrook carried the bomb into the drug store. Police feel most of them have no foundation."[57] Other newspaper accounts speculated, "What possessed him? Why did he do it? No one really knows, but the general feeling is that he believed that the store was responsible for his marital problems. If his wife was not working there, then she would be more dependent on him."[58] "Holbrook was known to be angry at Schieber and employees at Bingman's for 'coaching' her in marital matters." [59] Chief Temple declared in a newspaper article at the time, "There were too many unfounded rumors circulating...."[60]

Yet, stories have circulated for fifty years about who Phyllis Holbrook might have been having an affair with. I heard these tales. And so I asked everyone I interviewed about the rumors and if they could supply any truth to the gossip. Everyone had heard at least one story; yet, most people didn't put much credence in them. J.C. Penney's employee, Dennis Brown, remembered hearing rumors standing on the street while the buildings burned. But having talked to Patrolman Jack Mills on that day, Dennis maintained that the police did not believe any were true.

Folks told me wildly varying stories of who the affair was with. The list included Charlie Schieber, a pharmacist at a different drug store, a local philanderer with a "zipper problem," a man from Dayton, a local doctor, and my dad. Chief Temple had his own speculations, but his investigation into the event didn't require proving the private affairs of Phyllis. What was done, was done.

Karen Schieber also heard the rumors about her dad, and thought the same thing that I had all these years: If it were true that my dad was having an affair, did he somehow share some of the blame, too? I have had moments of doubts about my dad's loyalty without any way to prove them wrong. That's how vicious rumors take their toll.

These rumors were so universal that Chief Temple felt obliged to state, fifty years later when I first contacted him, "I just want to reassure you that both Ted and Charlie had better sense than to get messed up with that woman." Absolving my father and Charlie, but not absolving Phyllis. Another person summed it up for me, "You could tell who the gentlemen were in town, and who was not; and Charlie and Ted were gentlemen."

I have had to come to terms with these tales. After all my interviews, I have concluded that my dad was not having an affair. I was quite young at the time, but my parent's lives were so full and intertwined. They had five children, after all. I found it impossible to imagine an outside romantic interlude mixed into our daily lives.

Arnold Holbrook believed the same thing about his mom: "I don't think mom was having an affair. I think dad just kind of imagined it. I've heard the stories a hundred times, that my mom was having an affair with such and such. I never saw any evidence of anything. I was a teenager at the time. I think I was smart enough to figure things out. And I never saw anything of the kind. I think my dad mistook my mother's friendship with these people as having an affair."

From all that I have pieced together, I also don't believe Phyllis Holbrook was having an affair. Let that sink in. There was no affair. Maybe afterward, but not before. She was outgoing and friendly, and Holbrook was jealous and controlling. She knew many folks in town, including businessmen who frequented the restaurants and stores where she worked. But she was a mother first. She filed for divorce, perhaps because she was sick of being beaten by him, watching him beat her children, tired of the fear of his constant threats. She filed for divorce hoping for something better for her life. The final straw that shattered Holbrook's fragile ego may have occurred when police removed him from the home.

[]

I searched the archives of the Circleville Herald for the first mention of "domestic violence." I found it in a 1962 cartoon: a woman in an apron was violently jumping on the back of a man standing at the kitchen sink. The man was wielding a butcher knife facing the counter. It appeared that the woman was attacking the man from the back. The caption read, "This is NOT a scene of domestic violence – she's just protecting her new countertop from knife cuts!" [61]

I was horrified when I read this. Domestic violence was not a joke to me anymore.

I searched on, yet found very few newspaper references in 1967 to wife battery, wife beating, or women's shelters; but when I typed in "homicides," I was overwhelmed by the number of reports around the country where a "despondent husband" had killed his wife.

This wasn't new to Circleville, either. In a quick search of the archives of the local newspaper, I found a 1964 report of a Pickaway County murder of a wife and three others by her husband; and I found another one before that, in 1959.[62] This was not a rare occurrence. We just thought about it differently back then.

In 1967, wife-battering was not a crime. If the police were called to a home, they wouldn't get involved. Police needed to see severe injuries before they would consider an arrest. If it was written up, it might have been called a domestic disturbance. The first protection for women didn't come until 1979, when an Ohio law made wife beating, elderly abuse and other family-related violence an actual crime, punishable by a (whopping) maximum of six months in prison and a $1,000 fine.

Fifty years later, we have stronger laws, police training and support for survivors; yet, even so, statistics tell us that today, by the time you have read this paragraph, six people will have been battered in the United States. By this time tomorrow, two people in this country will die from their abuser's hand. Even more relevant to this story, a recent study of intimate-partner homicides "found that twenty percent of victims were not the intimate partners themselves, but family members, friends, neighbors, persons who intervened, law enforcement responders or bystanders."[63] The four people who died from Holbrook's deed, and the dozens who suffered physical and mental trauma from this event, these were the same bystanders, the casualties of domestic violence.

The "family" at Bingman's, including my dad, were friends who may have counseled and consoled Phyllis Holbrook about her abusive marriage and encouraged her to leave. Pervasive at the time, I found hints of stories of other women working at Bingman's who also coped with an abusive home life. Gratefully, today there are networks in almost every community, of women and men who risk their lives to help survivors of domestic violence leave their abusers, and help the survivors recover from self-blame, post-traumatic stress, and shock.

Even Holbrook's bomb idea was not unique. Before possession of dynamite was restricted in the early1970s, homemade bombs were common, I discovered through a slew of newspaper articles. Horrifyingly, as I searched the local newspaper for references to Holbrook, I found an article from September 1959 that mentioned Holbrook as a leader in his son's Cub Scout troop. To the left of this article was another titled: "Is American Woman Losing Femininity?" It was about the changing roles of men and women that "has resulted in some confusion, *but not danger*." (My italics added because the danger was obviously present.) On the right side of the Cub Scout article was a photograph with a headline about a woman in Seattle, Washington, who was "Blown to Bits by Home-Made Bomb" while she was sitting on her front porch. No motive was offered, but subsequent articles suggested that a "special friend" was to blame. I couldn't believe that on this one page I was staring at clues of the foretelling of Holbrook's actions.[64]

[]

All that Phyllis Holbrook lost that day was shocking. She was truly the unacknowledged sixth victim in this story. In many ways, except physically, she died with the explosion. Arnold filled me in on what became of his mom in the aftermath.

"She didn't deal with it. She went off the deep end. She…she was a mess," Arnold recounted. "A month later, my wife had our baby and we ended up moving in with my mom for a short time. But my mom went to Florida for a while. She had a sister there." When she returned, Arnold had moved his family to the nearby community of Kingston.

"A little while later, my mom moved away again. This time she disappeared. I found out where she lived maybe a year later. She was in Columbus. My mom had gotten a job at Lazarus (a popular department store). She lived in an upstairs apartment, with some little old landlady downstairs. I went upstairs and there was all that old furniture that came from the house on Mill Street. Everything. She had set up housekeeping. She was there for I don't know how long. But one day, she did not come back to the apartment. I kept getting phone calls from the landlady wanting to know where my mother was. I had no idea. She walked away and disappeared again. She left everything she owned in that old apartment. It was a nasty old place, dingy and dirty, probably all my mom could afford. I have no idea what happened to her, where she went, what she did. Nothing. My little brother stayed with my grandparents for a couple years. He didn't know where she went, either."

And then, out of the blue, Phyllis returned to Circleville. She had remarried. A horrible man by Arnold's measure. "I don't think the ink was dry on the marriage certificate before they were divorced. She was not married long."

Phyllis disappeared and reappeared several more times in her kids' lives. Arnold's wife, Edie, explained, "She was pretty good at that. She would leave. You didn't know where she went. You never heard from her. And then, suddenly, she was here."

"If my mother was still alive and you asked her where she went, I bet *she* couldn't tell you where she was or what she did. Her mind was totally gone," Arnold said. "I have a suspicion of what she did. She just bummed around, slept in hotel rooms and truck stops, and whatever. I think she just wanted to get away. I think she felt very, very ashamed of what had happened and I think she felt people blamed her. She just disappeared. I can just imagine what she did. Probably any place that had a motel room she would stay the night and then take off."

Fifty years ago, Phyllis Holbrook was about to be a divorcee. It was a time when, if you couldn't hold your family together, it was the woman's fault. If your husband "strayed," it was your fault. If your husband beat you, you must have deserved it. Lucky women married well.

Phyllis would remarry twice more, both men passing away relatively young. She would also have an acknowledged affair with a married man; her closest friends questioning why she would do that when she had been accused of the same behavior earlier with such devastating consequence. She was not lucky in love.

Phyllis Holbrook lived until she was eighty-seven and died on December 21, 2015, two months after my own mother's death.

She died in Circleville, ironically living at the same nursing home, at the same time, as my stepdad after my mother passed. Arnold reflected on her life: "I think Mom, when she passed away, had less at that time in her life than when we were kids. She had virtually nothing."

Arnold

Where do we get the idea that the sins of the father fall to the children? The answer is murky. The Bible tells us many times that each of us will make our own case at the Pearly Gates; and, yet, the fifth commandment states that "...for I the Lord your God am a jealous God, visiting the iniquity of the fathers on the children to the third and fourth generation for them that hate me."[65] Our lack of knowledge of who these people were may be what made us fear the children of this bad man. That's why we may have assumed that the family of this man would have moved away, vanished, fled.

But the fruits of the father, in this case, are not guilty. Holbrook's kids didn't conspire with him. In 1967, two of his children were already married and living their own lives, pointed in a different direction; minding their own business. His youngest son, fourteen years old and in high school, was devastated by his father's actions. It wasn't his children's fault. Yet, they felt the guilt, nonetheless.

"After the big event, I always thought people held it against me," Arnold said. "I felt like I had to keep on my best behavior, because people would always look at me with a different set of eyes than they would other people. I would go out of my way to be nice to people and tried to be an upstanding citizen so they wouldn't think something was wrong with me or it was my fault."

About six weeks after the event, Arnold's wife gave birth to a boy. The event weighed heavily on their marriage, and they eventually divorced, in 1972. "My first marriage went to hell.

My first wife, man, she got sucked into the mess big time and she really resented that. After a while, I quit visiting my son," he said.

Arnold and Edie married in 1974. Edie was thirteen when the Bingman's event happened. She was from a little farm near the village of Laurelville and remembered going into town with some girlfriends to look at the ruins. When she married Arnold, she didn't know who his dad was. A little while after her wedding, her boss asked, "Aren't you afraid of Arnold?" She asked "Why?" And he replied, "Because of what his dad did." And that's how she found out.

Arnold and Edie have led quiet lives. Retired now, they reminisced together about their thirty-year commute to their respective factory jobs in Washington Court House, about twenty minutes away. "Why didn't you ever move to Washington Court House?" I asked. "Arnie was a Circleville guy," Edie replied. "We bought our house and he never wanted to move."

"Those are my two kids, up there," and Arnold pointed to a framed picture of two twin dogs. "Best kids we ever had," he snorted; yet that wasn't completely true.

About three months after Arnold and Edie moved into their house, a single mom with four children moved in across the street. Through a series of tragic events, Arnold and Edie grew deeply attached to one of her sons. "When the neighbor child was only three years old, he would go out to the road and holler for me," said Edie. "I would go get him and walk him across the street to our house. He was here most of the time. He was here more than he was at home." There was a well-worn path between the boy's house and Arnold and Edie's heart.

When the boy was six, his mom and stepdad divorced. "His mom asked me if we wanted her son, and I said, well sure," Edie said. "Well, I thought we were going to get him and everything.

But when we went to court, Judge Ammer wouldn't let us have him because the stepdad got the house across the street. Judge Ammer said there would be turmoil here all the time. ...Some people in South Perry got him, but I would go down every Friday night to get him and then I would take him back on Sunday evening. Most of the time, we cried on our way back."

When the boy was fifteen, he was found living by himself in an old empty trailer at Else's Trailer Park. "Judge Ammer called and asked me, 'So Mrs. Holbrook, do you still want a boy?' And I said, 'Well, no, if we couldn't have that other one, I don't want another.' He said, 'Well it is that one.' Judge Ammer told me to meet him out there to Else's. So I did and he took me down to the trailer. He told the boy, 'You can't live here, you're too young. You have to go with Miss Holbrook.' With delight, Arnold and Edie helped this young man through high school, the Marines, two marriages, and an assortment of "grandchildren," one of whom was named after Arnold. "He still calls every day to see how we're doing." Edie added. "Friday's his day to mow my grass," Arnold said with a smile, talking over Edie in their enjoyment of the story.

"I had some bad times growing up, but I think that boy..." and Arnold whistled, "...he really had some bad times. I mean, I'm amazed the guy ain't in an insane asylum, I mean, or in prison. If I went through half of what he did, I'd been a total nut case."

I think the same thing about Arnold.

Jean

As the newspapers reported, Jean Schieber was in the hospital on the Saturday when the event occurred, recuperating from minor surgery the day before. The whole hospital was concerned about breaking the news to her, and when they finally told her, she was immediately sedated for a couple of days. She was released on Tuesday and the funeral was held the following day. Jean wrote about this moment in a letter to friends: "Having undergone surgery the previous day in our local Berger Hospital, I was spared the horrible sight of the downtown area till I could recover from the initial stages of shock."

Her son, Larry, remembered only a few things clearly about the day of the event. He was at a Cub Scout activity in another county on the day his dad died. His dad had dropped him off at Scoutmaster Jim Heacock's house that morning. Sometime in the afternoon, Mary Merriman, chaperone for the day and wife of the owner of the barbershop on Main Street just a few doors down from Bingman's, got a call. Larry remembered the adults talking in whispers; he heard a little of the conversation. "The barbershop was saved by the alley..." Larry knew something serious had happened. He was taken back to Circleville, to the hospital to see his mom. His sister was found and brought to the hospital, and that is where all three learned that their father was a hero. Larry wanted badly to see the store after the destruction, but nobody would take him downtown.

To this day, his sister, Karen, doesn't remember where she was. After all, she was only seven. She just remembered the family gathering, and the funeral, and then, "We went right back to school," she told me. "It was awkward and I was embarrassed.

I didn't know what to say. I was the only kid I knew from a single-parent home."

Jean Schieber knew no way but forward. At the end of the year, she wrote in her annual Christmas letter about her family's adjustments, seemingly to carry on with life as if the year had only contained a small hiccup or two.

> *"The children have done exceptionally well in adjusting. They have been a great help and indeed been my source of strength to go on. Larry immediately said he would take over the lawn for Daddy, which he did beautifully, as well as the cottage lawn and the lawn of one of the pharmacists at the store. Karen has, likewise, grown up so much and has done very well in accepting responsibility for a little girl of seven. They are both progressing nicely....He will be singing with the choir and Karen will be singing too with the second grade for their school Christmas program. Larry is in his third year of Cub Scouts and Karen is now a Brownie with all the enthusiasm that goes with scouting.*

These snippets of their life afterward conjured up a picture in my head of a train that, barreling down the road, hits a bump, jumps the track, and lands on a new track without missing a beat. The Schiebers just kept on going. Perhaps the family should have derailed, or perhaps it was the community that caught them, surrounding their engine, helping the wheels to touch down gently, and guiding all the cars that followed onto the new track.

Karen remembered her mom received "tremendous and ongoing support from the community -- friends, neighbors, church family, and Charlie's business colleagues." Jean had many very close women friends, "several of whom were like family members to us." But there was an impact. They just didn't know at the time what to look for.

Jean threw herself into the details of living. Hearing about the flurry of activity, it brought to mind the maxim "idle hands are the devil's workshop." Her frenzy masked the fear that if she slowed down, she would have too much time to think. She was a strong, stoic woman of German heritage, who worked very hard to go forward exactly as she and Charlie had planned.

Immediately after the funeral, Jean started working on the affairs of the drug store, dealing with the insurance company and helping the employees. The blast and fire had destroyed all but the store's goodwill. The insurance policies protected the merchandise and the wages of the employees for a time. The store space was leased, so the real estate loss was someone else's headache.

Jean made the quick decision to sell the "goodwill" of the store to Bob Scranton, Bingman's surviving pharmacist. Bob had pulled together a partnership with a businessman from Columbus to buy the store. Within thirty days, they had opened a temporary Bingman's Drug Store on the other side of Main Street while a new building was being constructed using the entire footprint of all three buildings destroyed in the fire. By September, the new Bingman's was opened. It was a modern, one-story building, built on the alley, which allowed a new feature: a drive-through prescription window. It also included a large parking lot on the west side of the building, where the original Bingman's store was located.

In her Christmas letter, Jean described the drive she felt for re-opening the drug store:

"Almost immediately, I found myself swept up in doing what I wanted more than anything -- to somehow reestablish

Bingman's Drugs as a memorial to Charlie and the other three who lost their lives in the tragic explosion. Through the combined efforts, much hard work, and concern of many, the store was reopened in a temporary location May 12. The doors of a beautiful new Bingman's Drugs opened to the public just two doors from the original location on September 25 with many of the same personnel. I am only in the store as a good Bingman customer and have been relieved of all responsibilities. I do, however, enjoy doing what I can in the way of public relations. The rebuilding and growth of the store has meant much to us and with Bob and Don's permission, the children still call it 'Daddy's store.'"

Many of the employees returned to work in the temporary store. Scott Lindsay, the stock boy, was among them. At first, Scott feared his college plans were over. But Jean Schieber and Bob Scranton made good on Charlie's pledge to help Scott go to pharmacy school. "It was a loan, and a Godsend to help me get through," said Scott. Bob also gave Scott the old Bingman's delivery station wagon to carry his things to Ohio Northern University, the alma mater of Bob, Charlie and Ted. The tradition would continue.[66]

The next point of business was rebuilding the cottage at Hargus Lake. Before the event, Jean and Charlie had drafted plans to rebuild their cottage that had been damaged by a tornado in February. Jean wrote: "During the summer, the children and I followed almost daily, the rebuilding of the cottage according to the original plans. With the kind help of a very competent contractor and close friend of Charlie's, we again have a cottage which we hope we will have the privilege of sharing with <u>many</u> of you next summer."

As if Jean didn't have enough to deal with, that summer her father fell seriously ill and remained in the hospital until "he was called to his Heavenly home" in November, leaving Jean's seventy-nine year old mother alone on the farm in Bucyrus (where she continued to live until the age of eighty-three). Jean's only sister lived in Cleveland. One can imagine the pressure and pull that Jean must have felt to move back home, to be closer to both. Like my mom, though, Jean decided to stay in Circleville. "She never remarried, and often said that no one could measure up to our dad," said her daughter, Karen. "She was devastated by the loss of her husband. She had waited for him for ten years before they were married and only had ten years of marriage before he was taken from her."

Larry and Karen don't recall receiving any professional help, individually or as a family, to deal with their loss. That's how it was for everyone I spoke to. You just dusted yourself off and moved on. Everyone tried to act like all was fine. Stay busy. Recounting the year in a Christmas letter in 1974, Jean wrote about a couple of tragic events that year that had impacted friends. "The combination of both have been grim reminders of April 15, 1967, but we don't ask why and count our many blessings. God has been so good to us. We carry on."

"My mom worked very hard to give us a normal childhood, a loving and accepting home. We traveled. We had a yard full of friends at our house all the time," Larry said. And he stayed busy too. In another Christmas letter, in 1973, Jean provided an exhausting list of activities that Larry, now sixteen and in high school, was involved in: choir, band, Key Club, DeMolay, a church usher, and he worked twenty-five to thirty hours per week at the store, "so I don't worry about his having something to do." Karen, at age thirteen, was no slacker, either. She was first chair piccolo in the Junior High School band, active in the church's youth ministry, took baton and piano lessons, and had five 4-H Club projects during the summer. The baton lessons paid off because the next year she won a coveted slot as a majorette for the Junior High School Band. She also added new activities in Latin Club, GAA, and Rainbow Girls, and helped in the church nursery.

The same year, Jean, Karen and Larry spent sixteen days in Europe, thanks to the generosity of Jean's mother. "It was the experience of a lifetime," Jean commented, sounding every bit put back together.

Yet she also mentioned in the same letter the problem with her voice that had started a year before. She had lost her voice for no apparent reason. Her voice was so compromised, she would carry a pen and paper everywhere she went. She couldn't even whisper, so she would write her words to the cashier at the grocery store.

She consulted with the Cleveland Clinic and the Mayo Clinic, with no clear results. The doctors decided it must be tension. Her voice was completely gone for many years, but it didn't slow her down. Even without a voice, Jean remained active, trying to teach the second-grade Sunday School class (and I scratch my head wondering how she did this), staying involved in the church's women circle and her teacher's sorority, Delta Kappa Gamma, and serving as treasurer of the Circleville Band Boosters. "With being so involved in activities," Jean noted, "I haven't really had a chance to follow through" on her speech therapist's treatment plan.

Finally, in 1976, Jean wrote: "In February it was necessary for me to get away for a complete rest so I spent three weeks with my sister and brother-in-law in Cleveland. Low and behold, during the third week there, I found my natural speaking voice coming back after about three and a half years of a real struggle with being able to talk." She eventually regained most of a normal speaking voice, but it was always weak and sounded strained, especially when she was under stress.

Larry, like his mother, had made plans when his dad was alive that steered him into his future. The only thing Larry ever wanted to be when he grew up was a pharmacist, like his dad. As he told me, "This was my 'Plan A' and I had no 'Plan B,' so it's a good thing that it has worked out well."

As Charlie Schieber's son, many of Charlie's friends and colleagues put their arms around Larry's shoulders and guided him to grow up into a solid man. His dad's legacy opened hearts and doors of business leaders in town.

By high school, he was well on the path that both Bob Scranton and Scott Lindsay had plotted, working as a stock boy at the new Bingman's Drug Store, under Bob's wings this time. After graduating from pharmacy school, Larry came home and worked for Bob again, this time as a pharmacist. Larry eventually opened his own pharmacy on the other side of town and became the spitting image of the quintessential community pillar that his father would have been so proud of.

Karen, on the other hand, was too young to have created a life plan before her father died. She just had activities and customs. She might have wanted to become a veterinarian, but it wasn't the custom in the day for women to pursue that field. When her mother's women friends put their arms around her, to mold her into the social norms allowed of women, it wasn't the same; she didn't feel their support. As Karen tells it: "Contrary to outward appearances, I had many struggles in high school, with much more than a small amount of teenage angst; anger at not having a father and the store tragedy; and rebellion against what I viewed at the time to be a very traditional mother. Fortunately, these struggles largely resolved after I left Circleville and went to college, but the store tragedy continued to haunt and affect me for many years."

She had to find her own way. She went to college and became a nurse, not a teacher like her mom, yet still on the list of acceptable careers for women. (Interestingly, Jean Schieber had wanted to pursue a career in nursing, but her father wouldn't let her at the time, fearing she would be drafted into the military.) I might be projecting from my own experience about how hard it might have been for Karen to finally come into her own person, to veer off the path that her father would have understood for her. She could fight with her mother, but how do you fight with the expectations of a ghost?

Keeping with the social path to happiness as defined by her mother's generation, Karen married a doctor and had lovely children. "I like to think that my mom thought the best thing I ever did in my life was to marry my husband, not because he was a doctor, but because he made me happy. What more could any mother want for her children."

Yet, a few years later, rebelling from the stereotype of "nurse marrying the doctor," Karen went back to school and became an attorney.

"In later years, I became very close to my mother and I eventually grew to realize, appreciate and admire what a strong, smart and determined woman she was. I feel that going through such adversity helped to shape me into a very strong and determined person, too." It's hard to pinpoint exactly how the event shaped her, but Karen believes it helped her develop a spirit of ultimate preparedness: "I always feel compelled to prepare myself for the worst possible outcome in any significant life event. I don't view this as a bad thing. If I am prepared for the worst, I will be equipped to deal with whatever comes. If the source of my determination, preparedness and strength is related to the tragedy, at least some positive things have resulted."

When Karen and I sat down to talk about the past, we started by catching up with our lives. She matter-of-factly told me about the long-distance bike trips her husband and she liked to take. They rode their bikes all over Ohio, which sounded fun. And then she told me they had once ridden their bikes from Cincinnati to Bucyrus and Mansfield, almost two-hundred miles, to visit her mom and dad's graves. I was impressed. She next shared that they had also pedaled from Cincinnati to Vermont, a thousand-mile journey. The trip started in the pouring rain. I was in awe. And just as plainly, she told me of the family vacation to Tanzania to climb Mt. Kilimanjaro. This wasn't normal. I admired her, but this wasn't what most Ohioans aspired to. And I thought, "You go, girl. Keep moving forward, but break the mold."

Chuck

It took me forever to track down Chuck Willison, the only remaining spouse of one of the victims of the event. I didn't know him; and my family didn't know his family. I kept chasing every lead until I found a friend of a friend who blindly, but graciously, gave me his phone number. When I called him, he invited me to his house, a few miles out of town. The same house he had built with Francis more than sixty years past.

The day I interviewed Chuck, he had just come in from the yard. At eighty-six, Chuck had the look of a kindly old-geezer in his blue jeans and flannel shirt. He had spent the better part of the day outside, taking down a tree. He had made a deal with his barber. "Free hair cut for the fire logs," he said with a proud snort.

Chuck lived by himself. To look around his house, you might think he was frozen in time. The home was simple and clean, yet I got the impression that it looked very much like it did fifty years before. The paint may well have been the same; the furniture and rugs showed years of wear.

Chuck sat comfortably in a squeaky recliner, positioned strategically in front of an old television, with an ottoman next to him doubling as a side table that held his remote control and a pistol in a holster (for late night protection, I assumed). I could imagine he had spent many a night over the past five decades in this same position.

He was happy to have company, someone interested in hearing about his life. "I've never spent this much time talking about what happened, never to nobody," he told me in his slightly too-loud and strong voice. He was a bit hard of hearing, and although he wore hearing aids, he was not used to them yet. "They tickle my ears," he said.

Back in the day, Chuck knew Phyllis Holbrook by face from the drug store, but he didn't know her husband. "Good thing he was killed or I would have gone after him," said Chuck. "I remember talking to Lonnie Lagore after the event. He was mad at Holbrook, just like me." Chuck told me his stories of the war and his prowess as a hunter and I realized he wasn't just spouting off.

"After the event, I heard tales, rumors, that she (Phyllis) was messing around with Charlie Schieber. I knew Charlie Schieber and his wife and I didn't believe it. I think I knew him better than that." Chuck didn't recall rumors before the event, about Phyllis and another man. "It was a shock to everybody. People said Holbrook thought she was fooling around, but how he got that impression, I don't know.

"Back in the day, I knew some people who were members of the Eagles. After the event, I talked to a couple of guys who I knew fairly well. They told me that Holbrook had been in the Eagles that morning, drinking, and he had a box that looked like a cigar box[67] that had five sticks of dynamite in it. They told me, 'When he left, we didn't know what he was going to do or where he was going to go, but we knew he was going to do something.' I don't remember who they were; they were older than me at that time, so they're probably gone by now. I remember telling them, 'You probably should have stopped him.'"

He was left to raise his sons on his own. "It was hard, but they were boys, thank goodness. I didn't have to explain the girl part. My kids, evidently, got along with me well enough. My brother's daughter, Judy, and her husband lived next door, and she helped a whole lot."

He also never remarried. "I just didn't feel like I wanted some other woman coming in acting and pretending to be their mother. She couldn't be. I didn't want that when the kids were young. I can't explain why, but I just didn't want it. After the kids left, after they were on their own, there was one woman that I dated a few times, but it never went anywhere."

Chuck had worked at Wardell's Carpet and Rugs, which, adjacent to Bingman's, was also destroyed by the blast and fire. Mr. Wardell rebuilt the store in a new location, on North Court Street, and Chuck continued to work for him until Wardell sold out at the end of 1983. "I went to work one morning and he told me I could go home. He had sold the place. For almost thirty years I crawled around the floor like a little baby," Chuck said, without any malice or resentment. "Folks ask me how my knees are. I don't have a bit of problem with my knees. It's my lower back that gets tired," he said, without complaint.

In the ensuing years, Chuck lost two of his three sons: Gary, to a car accident ("Well, a minivan and a semi-truck can't be at the same place at the same time, and he was killed instantly," Chuck explained) and Rick, to a heart attack while training to run marathons.

His last son, Jim, lived in Indiana and was one of the last people I interviewed, via a Skype video call. It was my longest interview. Jim was so willing to talk, and more than anything, he wanted to ask me questions, to learn more about the details of the event. The Willison's lived about five miles east of town and they had gone to county schools in the Logan Elm school district. Jim didn't know my family or the Schieber's or anyone else in this story, for that matter. "I'm almost ashamed of how little I know about the event," he told me.

Sadly, Jim was so young, that he didn't have many memories of his mom, either. He recalled the details of that day, but her personality and what she was like, what she would have thought, he doesn't remember much. "I have memories that we ate dinner around the table, and a few other things, but mostly memories in our old house. She lived in the new house for just a couple of years. I remember her being there, but I don't remember *her*. I remember brief instances being in the room with her, maybe some comments, but to say that I knew her, no." And he added, "When I die, and get to Heaven, the first ten thousand years I want to spend just getting to know her again, and then I'll figure out what I'm going to do with the rest of my time."

At eight years old, Jim didn't really understand what was going on. "I remember being at the funeral home, seeing a box, and asking my dad, 'Is that where Mom is?' It was probably fifteen years later that Dad had a jeweler put the diamond from her wedding ring into his ring; and during that process, I saw mom's charred watch and ring that they had recovered from the fire; and that is when I finally realized that she was in the crux of the explosion."

The funeral was on Wednesday after the event. Jim remembered parts of the funeral, especially wondering why his friends were there. "It wasn't because second-graders wanted to be there," he said, "but because their parents had taken them." Jim and his brothers were probably out of school for the entire week. "I remember going back to school and thinking, 'I've been out too long. I should have gone back to school a little earlier,'" Jim said. "You go back and you assume everybody is looking at you. Everybody is staring at you." But he wanted to get back to the comfort of a familiar routine.

His memories, like most of the people I interviewed, were sketchy for quite a while after the event. I asked him when his memories resumed and he said, "It would have been either that summer or the following summer. Rhoades Farm Market was down the road from our house. My older brother Rick had taken a job as a clerk in the market and they needed strawberry pickers. We picked strawberries, then green beans, then we picked lima beans and sweet corn and pumpkin; and then school started. I enjoyed that work. There were four of us that worked the fields. I remember one of the other field hand's dad had died. He came from a big family. They had less than we did, and we didn't have anything. That job was probably the thing that got me moving forward and not wallowing."

No one helped him or his family "process" the event. "I would imagine there were people who stepped in and did what they could, not professional counselors, but people at the church who had a close enough walk with God that they could share things with me. Yet, to say someone formally sat down with me, no," Jim said.

"When my dad came home from Korea, he had a long boat ride home, enough time to think about what he had seen and done, but no formal counseling around the things that had happened there. They didn't talk about PTSD[68] back then. Because of that, my dad may have brought a little of the Korean War syndrome to this tragedy. His mantra was, 'I can't "un-see" this, I can't undo this, but I can go forward.' I learned that I can change what today is. That's the way we progressed. We didn't talk a lot about it. As an adult, I never had a conversation about the event with my brothers."

But Jim didn't feel alone. He had his brothers and his dad and his Uncle Bob. "My cousin, who lived next door, stepped in mightily. Not like mom, nowhere near like that, but, you know, I always thought that she had my back. And people at church. We knew we were "that kid", but we also knew there were people who supported us.

"One thing I regret is that I don't know my mom's family, because nobody reached out. I was too young. I knew the one sister, but my mom had seven siblings. I couldn't tell you their names; I didn't get to know them except the one sister who came down, Mildred and her husband, George. They had three boys and a girl. They invited us to their home in Columbus. I can see their house in my mind. When you visit someone's house, that matters. Like, you now know my dad because you visited his house," Jim told me and I nodded in understanding.

"When my younger brother died, his kids, my nephews, were very young. I have made a point to call them every year. They don't always talk to me. They don't always return my calls or they call me back when they are good and ready. But if they ever wanted to know about their dad, my brother, they know who to call. If my nephews don't know the Willison family, it's not for my lack of trying. I have seen to that. Because I feel -- not cheated -- but I wish my mom's family had reached out more. I know it was harder back then. But there's no excuse that they didn't pick up the phone and call every now and then like Mildred did. So, I've taken a completely different approach with my nephews having gone through a similar situation." This is both sad and beautiful to me as I thought about how hard it was today to keep my family together and our collective memories alive.

Just a few years ago, Jim took his teenaged daughter with him to a meeting in Circleville, at the courthouse. "Of course, you don't leave town without going to Lindsey's (Bakery) for a donut," Jim said. "We walked up the alley, to Main Street. And suddenly, I became vividly aware that we were across the street from where Bingman's Drug Store had been. I remember being there with my daughter, and at that moment, I realized she didn't know anything about what had happened. She only knew that my mom had been killed in an accident. I shared with her, right there on the street, what happened," and Jim's strong, baritone voice went just a little unsteady.

"I guess I don't share it often because people don't ask. And if they don't ask, do they care? It's something many don't remember. I haven't said anything to my older daughter, because, it's just one of those things like... I can tell you why TDMA modulation on your cell phone is better than FDMA, but do you care? No. You just want to pick up a cell phone and make a call. And that's kind of how I look at this. If someone wants to know, I'll talk all day. But if you don't care, I'm not going down that road. I shared this deep thing with my daughter that day, briefly, and I would guess that she might not even remember being there or anything I said. But that was the one time I spoke of it, when it gave me pause to talk about it, to be standing in front of the memory like that."

[]

When Chuck moved to Circleville in 1952, he was building a community around him. His mom and dad, his brother and family, their new church community, his wife and three sons. This was what life was supposed to hold for him. Fifty years later, alone now, Chuck had outlived most of his community. Chuck observed that "life was great before that happened," but he didn't seem bitter or sad. His strategy for moving on, he said, had been to put a lot of it out of his mind. "I'll never forget that she was killed. It's impossible to do that. I just don't have anything to do with that part of my life anymore. I've tried to ignore it completely. You just try to forget the bad things. You had a father that was killed. I had a wife. You never forget, but you try to forgive. You forgive people for doing the thing. She was killed in a freak accident and we just accepted it."

Chuck talked to me matter-of-factly about all these pieces in his life. Talking to him in person that day, he seemed clear-headed, solid, a happy man. Yet, when I had a chance to step back and add it all up, I thought, "Wow, what a hard life." Yet, Jim set me straight about his father. "If we had my dad's funeral tomorrow, I would tell whoever was doing the funeral, don't talk about the bad stuff. People talk too much about that, what he's been through. That's not who my father is or how he has lived his life.

"My dad was selected last year to go on an Honor Flight, where military veterans get on a plane at four in the morning, fly to Washington D.C. They show them all the monuments and memorials, and fly them back the same day. Part of the process was to ask family and friends to write letters to the veteran. I asked family members to write letters, and I asked them just to thank him for his service. That's all they needed to say. Don't bring up all the hard stuff. We don't need to go there. Just thank him for his service."

Chuck summed it up that day I sat with him. "I've been through a lot, but on the other hand, I've had a good life. I've been very fortunate. It's part of the call of being a religious person. You just hand it over to the Lord. He can't make things *not* happen, but He can help you through."

With that, at the end of our conversation, Chuck invited me to see his make-shift trophy room with antlers mounted on the walls from deer, antelope, and even a caribou from northern Quebec. "I do a little hunting," he reminded me, and he showed me a bunch of pictures of his family.

Lonnie

In 1967, Lawrence (Lonnie) and Martha (Mart) Lagore had been married for twenty-seven years. He was not well-loved by Mart's family, having started out on the wrong foot by eloping with her to Kentucky in 1939. They had two children, Gary and Linda. Gary was living in Circleville with his wife, whom he had married in 1965, right after returning from Vietnam, decorated with his war wounds and a Purple Heart. Linda at the time was also married and living with her growing family in Mississippi.

Lonnie worked at one of Circleville's factories. His claim to fame in Circleville was his passion for bowling on his team, the *Courthouse Barbershop*. He was honored with a big write-up in the local newspaper in 1962 when he broke the all-time high record at Prairie Lanes, coming up "thirteen points shy of a perfect game, spilling only seven pins on his second ball in the tenth frame. His third ball of the final frame cleaned the three remaining pins for a spare."[69] While this may seem trivial to some, it was important enough to be mentioned five years later in a "Looking Back in Pickaway County" section of the newspaper.

The after-story for Lonnie was almost impossible to put together, as he and his children have all passed on to their glory. The only verifiable information I could uncover was that he remarried two years later, to his son's mother-in-law.

Lonnie and Mart's grandchildren, niece and nephew live on, but in other towns, in other states, and with limited connection to the place and time when life seemed normal. I spoke with Mart's granddaughter and a niece, but their stories about Lonnie were a blend of grade-school memories and second- and third-hand family lore passed down from the unfavorable perspective of Mart's family.

[]

I reflected on my own family, so large and multigenerational. We were once so involved in our town; yet, today, only one brother remains in Circleville. I stopped to consider: *Does our next generation, my nieces and nephews, know this story?* And I realized for the first time how short life really is and how a family's history can be lost in an instant, like a virtual file that disappears from a computer's memory bank. It will just cease to exist if we don't somehow preserve it.

.

Eileen

In the flash of the explosion, my mom found herself a single parent with five children. When she was married in the early 1950's, she had built her dreams on the assumption of long-term companionship, of an ideal marriage. My mom and dad had built their life on a foundation of love and a strong sense of what society considered to be wifely and husbandly duties, beyond who cooked dinner and who took out the trash. She had gladly given him all the children he wanted and then some, to fill his hole of being an only child. And now these kids and their life were her sole responsibility.

In the new beginning, my grandmother (my mother's mother) wanted my mom to move back home, to Portsmouth, and live with her. Grandpa had died in 1964 of a heart attack, and my grandmother lived alone, but within blocks of her sisters, nieces, nephews, uncles and aunts. It was likely that my mother realized the friends she had made in Circleville offered more opportunity than her family and a life in Portsmouth. What's that saying? You can't go home.... After all, my mom's two sisters had also left Portsmouth after high school, looking for a better life. They had settled in Washington, D.C., and New Orleans with their new families. The sisters stayed in touch, but it meant letters in lieu of expensive long-distance telephone calls on a party line. And, from time to time, each made the lengthy car trip to visit.

My other grandmother (my dad's mom) had been a widow for a decade. Even before her only son died, she had lived a quiet, retiring life in Sciotoville, knitting booties and cooking lunch at the local elementary school. She was perfectly experienced with taking care of herself, seeming to enjoy living alone; or maybe she lived with a heavy heart over her solitude, without her husband and now without her only son. We loved to go visit. She allowed us kids to ramble from top to bottom of her house. We grandkids brought her joy, and she was a wonderful grandmother to us. But she wasn't a "mother" to my mom. The two were more like friends who shared the memories of my dad; widowed adults, together trying to get by, and they shared a deep love for five funny, rambunctious kids.

My mom chose to stay in Circleville. It takes a village, they say, and for us it was the beloved community who stepped in that first year to help my mom adjust. I will never know all the ways they helped, but I know when I shut my eyes and picture each of our neighbors at the time, I see their serious and laughing faces taking care of us and showing us love. I have lost memories, the details of life immediately following the event. But there is proof that our family survived; we moved on.

On reflection, my practical side wanted to understand how my mother managed financially to take care of her family. My mom was smart; she was financially savvy; and she was from the generation of hardy stock who were sometimes called "Depression Babies," meaning she had learned the hard way how to stretch a nickel. She was left with a life insurance policy and insurance from Bingman's, which paid my father's monthly salary for a while. My dad was a veteran, so there were monthly benefits for his wife and children (and later, help with college), and monthly Social Security death benefits for the children. All in all, it was a decent monthly income in that day. My mom and dad had paid less than $20,000 for their three-bedroom ranch-style home, and it was almost paid off. A loaf of bread cost twenty-five cents, chicken was twenty-seven cents a pound, and a gallon of milk was fifty cents. She may not have trusted it at the time, but my mother would be okay financially.

The tougher question for my mom was not whether she could make it on her own, but how would she maintain the lifestyle to which she had become accustomed? She didn't want to move backward socially; she cherished her "position" in Circleville. She was surrounded by people on the social ladder she aspired to. But she wasn't married. Her adult social life would change.

My mom was a strong-willed woman in an era hugging the border of convention and liberation. When my mom graduated from high school in the 1940s, she had three choices that would maintain her reputation as a lady: teacher, secretary or nurse. My mom chose to be a nurse. Social convention in the 1950s led my dad to insist that my mom not work outside of the home. Yet, my mom stayed connected to her profession in the ways acceptable to my dad and society, by volunteering her talents at the Well-Child Clinic, the Hospital Guild, the Red Cross and as an active member of the Pickaway County Registered Nurses Association, hosting meetings at her home filled with other stay-at-home registered nurses.

Luckily for my mom, by the late 1960s, women around the country were talking about reforms and there was growing sisterly support for women to work outside of the home and earn their own living. My mom was not a feminist marching in the street. She didn't meet with other women in town to plot the overthrow of the system that kept women oppressed. She actually looked down on these "F" word[70] activists. She was a lady who had been raised on female convention, loved to shop, get her hair and nails done, and dress up. Paradoxically, my mom would ultimately benefit from the women's movement of the 1960s, as much as her life was devastated by the backlash from a man (Holbrook) who couldn't handle those changes. Her unfortunate situation occurred at an important crossroad in history, and she was able to capitalize on the progress being made to serve her family well. So it isn't surprising that after my dad died, she enrolled in a nursing refresher course developed especially for registered nurses who had interrupted their careers to have babies. She easily found part-time work at the local welfare department and the hospital after that.

Life without my father was hard, and tending to five children was exhausting. She became both our mother and our father, being gentle and nurturing one minute and suddenly stern and tough the next, which for us kids looked frazzled and out of control as she lost her cool and yelled at us. While we knew that our dad was gone, we had little concern for how we needed to modify our expectations now that we had only one parent. We continued to demand, as kids do, that every one of our daily needs be met. We didn't give my mom a break. In fact, we were needier than before. We asked in a thousand ways for our mom to fill our hole, to be our whole. We were just kids.

Two years after the event, my mom started to make new life decisions for our family, beginning with moving into town. With my sister starting high school, my mom needed relief from the constant carpooling and chauffeuring of kids who lived five miles out of town. We bought a four-bedroom, two-story house in the same neighborhood where the Osborns had lived, within walking distance to the three different schools the five kids attended – elementary, junior high and senior high. Again, I wondered how she did that. Extending credit to women wasn't customary at the time. But, once again, our family friend, Earl Palm, at Second National Bank, helped. "We did things differently back then. We didn't have all the regulations," Earl said modestly. "If we knew someone, we wanted to help them out." He helped a lot of people back when small-town banking was based on relationships.

Our new house was also within walking distance of the hospital, where my mom eventually worked part-time, so she could pop home unexpectedly or be home quickly if needed. She worked in the emergency room, where tough nurses were given a lot of critical care responsibilities, working shoulder to shoulder with doctors. My mom was okay-looking, not a dashing beauty. She was short at five-foot-three, and her figure had been ravished by the labor of five kids. But she had a great smile, liked to laugh, and talked to everyone. Living in a small town, working in a hospital, these were the makings of a steamy script for the famous primetime soap opera "Peyton Place." My mom once told my sister, as an adult, "You would be surprised at all the men who propositioned a widow." Yet, as far as I know, my mom kept her cherished Christian values intact during this time.

As if moving wasn't chaotic enough, without completely unpacking our things, my mom boldly took us five kids on the summer vacation of a lifetime, driving our station wagon cross-country to California, sightseeing the whole way: New Mexico, the Painted Desert, the Grand Canyon, and Las Vegas, specifically to see the casino-performing heartthrob of the time, Wayne Newton. We went to the San Diego Zoo, Disneyland, and Lake Tahoe. My mom drove the whole way, as none of the kids were old enough to have a driver's license. The youngest was five, the oldest was fourteen. We must have been gone for three weeks or more. We stayed an extra week in Santa Cruz, where my mom became ill with adult tonsillitis -- or maybe she was just exhausted from the trip and life. My sister was put in charge of us kids, and I remember running helter-skelter all over the famous boardwalk and amusement park, while my mom stayed in our motel apartment with the curtains closed and the lights out. She recovered after a week, and we were no worse for wear as we continued our journey.

It would become clearer at the end of her life that my mother loved to travel, but in the moment, this trip seemed like a crazy idea. Was she on her way to insanity? Had she dealt with her grief? Was her illness more of a mental breakdown? I can only imagine what my grandmothers, aunts, and the neighbors thought of this journey, especially when they got the phone call that she was sick. More practically, how was she able to manage buying a house and financing a wild vacation for six? Except, she was smart like that. Looking back, though, it was a good idea, a great idea. I learned by example that women don't have limits. It bonded our family together and was the spark we needed to start our memories again. I couldn't tell you anything that happened between my dad's death and that trip, but I have vivid memories of singing songs in the car, walking on the beach, and starting sixth grade.

We came home, settled into our new routine, in our new house, and life moved forward. While we kids knew that my mom had been spending time with one of our former neighbors, it came as a bit of a shock when she announced in 1971 that she was going to marry this widower with five kids who lived in Knollwood Village. Of course, we knew the family. We had played many a game of croquet in their back yard. However, combining the two already large families seemed a bit much. It wasn't necessary.

I have often wondered why she remarried in this crazy way, taking on so much more responsibility. Was love that strong? As I pieced together the timeline for this project, I realized that my grandmother, my mom's mother, had died in October 1970, young at seventy and unexpectedly from a stroke. I can now imagine the grief and the fear my mom may have felt, of truly being on her own with five kids. Maybe that swayed her into agreeing to the proposal of marriage. They announced their engagement in January 1971 and were married in June.

During the six months in between, we remodeled our house in town, carving out two bedrooms and a fourth bathroom from the former garage, adding a seventy-five-foot-long back section for a bigger dining and family room and a new two-car garage. Combining our homes took enormous effort outside of the practicalities of moving in two refrigerators, two washers, two dryers, and a full-sized drinking fountain. The Foster kids were independent, strong-willed, and sarcastically funny as our way of enduring our tragedy. The new kids were subdued, sadder because the loss of their mother to cancer was more recent, and much more reverent about their situation. We were from the hills; they had lived in Europe.

My mom was well-known for saying our family had "yours, mine, but no 'ours,'" as a riff off the title of a popular movie about a blended family. Yet our blending was not smooth. The ages of the ten kids dovetailed, so that both sides were spread throughout the lineage and none were in the same grade in school. But, also spread throughout, were different customs, different manners, and different personalities. I inherited a throw pillow from my mom that summed up my mom's style of governance in the house: "I'm not bossy, I just have better ideas!" On hindsight, unsurprisingly, my mom was constantly exasperated by how hard it was to enforce her will.

Our new stepdad went to work every day and left the kids and domestic chores to my mom. He was mainly a good guy, but quiet in the house. He was an engineer who tinkered in the garage with the six boys and taught them how to fix cars and ride motorcycles. He took us water skiing, and then disappeared when the day-to-day chores of raising kids resumed.

There are many stories, the highs and the lows, to be told about those years, yet, suffice it to say, at the end of the day, the marriage, our blended family, and our hard-fought love for each other lasted for forty-five years.

Yet in a surprising twist, at the end of their lives, my mom and stepdad made the decision to be buried next to their respective, original spouses, the mother and father of their biological children. The bond to the former life had not been forgotten. It was merely put aside until they could be reunited in Heaven.

Joni

I felt I couldn't end this story without some account of how this tragedy affected my life. I could start by blaming a few quirks in my personality on the event. I'm very afraid of fire. I'm always smelling smoke. I worry that just around the bend could be a horrible, deadly surprise, especially when I'm not expecting it, so I try to stay hypervigilant. It comes up a lot when I'm flying, when I'm not in control.

Yet, I recognized that I couldn't conclusively tie superficial tics to my father's death, just as I couldn't make a definitive connection to deeper impacts that this tragedy may have had on me. There are too many competing factors to say for sure that this one event changed everything, or even changed anything. It is difficult to tease it out, to say, "I'm like this today *specifically* because of that trauma." But if I were to describe the impact the event had on me, it might be that the box that kept the knowledge of what was normal or possible in life was shattered in the explosion; my emotions lost their boundaries. Would I have been the same person regardless, and pushed the edges of social norms? Who knows, and it ultimately doesn't matter; but this is how I made sense of the connection.

After the event, I continued to grow up in a loving household, surrounded by family and friends. We continued breathing in and out the picturesque life of a small town. All was well, right? Or so it would seem.

I was called a "sensitive" kid growing up. It meant I cried a lot. So, when my dad died so suddenly and tragically, at first I was very sad sometimes. I started sharing a bedroom with my mom so she wouldn't be lonely, and, so, I had a front-row seat watching my mom be very sad. She leaned heavily on me with her worries even at my young age. I didn't know what to do with my own emotions, much less what to do with hers. You could say I was full of emotion: my mom's and my own.

The byproduct of trauma is that some people are driven to recreate recurring situations that produce extreme emotions, putting them on dramatic highs and lows. Other people are driven to stay clear of their emotions and pursue as unemotional a life as possible. I was the kid who sought out the highs, and got some of the lows as a sad bonus.

When my mom remarried and we added five more kids to the mix, I moved back into my own bedroom and receded into the woodwork at home as many middle children can. There were so many of us that chaos often ruled. The rest of my life may have had more to do with our expanded family dynamics, but the seeds of change were planted at my dad's death.

I came into consciousness in the 1970s, meaning I started having memories again. I was mesmerized by the Age of Aquarius and entranced by the idea of *hippies* and rock 'n' roll. In my teens, I quickly and wholeheartedly embraced a life of drinking and partying. I was part of a large group of friends; specifically, a large group of teenage girls who let their hair down in high school, in college and into adulthood.

Many of my high school friends were a year ahead of me, and my sisters were all older, leaving me with a house full of brothers and stepbrothers. Anticipating my situation, in my junior year of high school I pleaded with my mom to let me go to a boarding school in Virginia for my senior year. I won't ever know why she also thought it was a good idea -- perhaps to calm the chaos in our house, perhaps to get me away from bad influences -- but she let me go. Yet I carried my life with me, and, not surprisingly, I was expelled from the school for four days for drinking. This might have indicated that something was amiss, but kids will be kids, and I wasn't alone in the weekend of debauchery.

My first year of college, I went to a renowned party school in North Carolina, where I made quick friends with wild girls eager to skip whole weeks of classes to hitchhike around the region to different party sites. I almost flunked out, and scared myself by how much I was partying and the risks I was willing to take. So, in a moment of clarity, I moved back to Ohio and enrolled at The Ohio State University, closer to my mom and family who might keep a better eye on me. They didn't. They couldn't imagine what I was up to.

Somehow, though, I managed to graduate from college. My curiosity about the world, combined with having no idea of what to do next, led me to the Peace Corps and Africa. I learned beautiful lessons about how others lived, struggled and played. Unfortunately, I took my drinking problem with me, which came in handy when I was overwhelmed with emotions and the stress of waking up every day seeing, smelling, and touching an exotic world that had no ties to my upbringing. I have vivid memories of buying fish off a woman's head, staring down a green mamba snake, and spying on the men's secret society meeting in the jungle, all with a beer in my hand. I left Africa in the first year because I had another moment of clarity to the chaos and risks I was taking, and I scared myself into leaving.

I moved to California to live near my sister. I eventually went to graduate school, still partying. However, through my new network of friends in the counseling department, I started learning a little about dealing with loss, grief and feelings. At the age of thirty-one, through the fellowship of Alcoholics Anonymous, I heard for the first time people talking out loud about the bad things that had happened in their life. About shame and fear, and other overwhelming emotions. I started to learn that I didn't have to drown my feelings with alcohol, but it would take me awhile to learn what to do with my feelings without alcohol.

My next step was to set out, sober this time, to chase exotic highs. I spent almost three years in Nicaragua, working in rural, remote villages to dig wells for clean drinking water. This was a dangerous time in Nicaragua, right after the war, when some hundred-thousand men were decommissioned from the army, with no jobs available, and soldiers were allowed to keep their rifles. In parts of the country, it resembled the Wild West. I was living on my own, and seemingly doing well until one day I had a third moment of clarity. I was visiting back in the States, driving in the peaceful hills of California's Sonoma Valley, when I realized that I wasn't on constant high alert, looking up ahead for a dust cloud signaling a vehicle coming toward me that might be armed. I realized in that moment that, in Nicaragua, I was living off adrenaline in place of alcohol, and losing, once again, my ability to assess risk. So, once again, I returned home to Ohio.

Ultimately, looking back, I have great memories and feel blessed for the opportunities I have had in life. Sometimes I was wild, frantic, and living on the edge, but mostly I saw it as trying to live boldly, to "break the mold." The only parts that I wish had been different were the times when, so obvious now, I was reacting to hidden emotions rather than guiding my own destiny. Too many times I was on a roller-coaster, acting like I wasn't afraid of anything, but, in truth, I was a scared nine-year-old.

Today I am settled on a little farm in Texas with a man who told the world when he recited his wedding vows to me that I was the sanest person he knew. He wasn't around during the crazy parts, so I take that as the compliment he intended, that I have mellowed nicely. He has also taught me about setting boundaries, how to calm my nervous rub, how to enjoy a steady, lackluster life, and to work out my emotions in a healthy way sweating in my garden.

Still, every time I get into an emotional crisis, my first response is to fantasize about exotic places I haven't been, and plan how I can get there, to escape. This past year, I have dealt with the losses of my mother and stepfather, and the intense memories of this story. Every step of the way, I have made plans for hundreds of exotic trips -- Argentina, Spain, Ethiopia -- pathways to escape these feelings. I gave myself permission to take those trips if I needed to. But I know from experience, now, that it's the coming home that tears me up, when I finally must face my fears. So, today, I generally just stay put.

[]

In my thirties, I had the opportunity to chat with an old high school classmate. I hadn't known him well, but I knew the family because they lived down the street. I watched from the sidelines as his quintessential family went to church, were leaders in Boy Scouts, and continued with higher education. They lived in a nice house on a perfect street, and their dad had a good job. I thought I knew who this family was. I had imagined what life was like in a "normal" family. Yet, he told me a different story of his family's internal struggles, one of heartache and fights and runaway children and rejection of each other.

My friend was also mad at his parents in the same way I was mad at mine at the time. We complained about the same things, that they wouldn't listen, wouldn't talk about things important to us. We seemed to have opposite views of the world from our parents. He described his parents' views in a way that I thought only my mom and stepdad held, because we were "different." I understood at that moment that the "odd" ways of my parents were, really, not that different than their peers. I realized that what I had experienced growing up was also entangled with the proverbial generation gap, an era when society had broad-leaped ahead with social changes greater than prior generations had weathered. Looking back, I wondered how we didn't lose more to all the social upheaval. Yet, new opportunities abounded: education, birth control and the power of women to break out of a mold, question authority and rebel. So, I can't completely attribute the choices I have made in my life to my original trauma, but the event at Bingman's Drug Store is the moment when *the butterfly flapped its wings* for me and life dramatically changed.

Halfway through writing this book, I became acutely aware that, once again, I was pushing myself to the brink of overwhelming emotions in a way that normal folks would instinctively avoid. Yet, I pushed on. Paradoxically, hearing the story told and retold to me has ultimately freed me of its overwhelming power. The havoc caused by the butterfly is starting to feel less intense, more like a momentary ripple in an otherwise calm and good life.

We have a lithograph hanging in our house of a giant mountain with steps carved out of the boulders and silhouettes of people in various stages of climbing up. At the bottom of the mountain are many people who haven't even started the journey -- people of the abyss. Some of the silhouettes have taken their first step, some are halfway up, others are resting, out of breath, climbing with balls and chains tied to their ankles, babies in their arms, tackling a boulder too big. A few have made it to the top; and a few are reaching back with a hand for others.

I have seen myself at different times of my life at different places on this mountain, sometimes tackling higher boulders, sometimes offering a hand to others, and other times sitting with someone on the lower rung, providing encouragement to move forward. Today, I'm somewhere in the middle of the mountain of life, right where I need to be, quietly sitting on a step, staring out into the horizon, not looking up or down. My heart is warm, but also overflowing with both the good and the bad of this story, and I need time to process it. I'll get up soon enough, and start climbing again. But right now, I just want to sit, and take a little time to think about the past.

ACKNOWLEDGMENTS

This book is the product of our collective memories. I am forever grateful to the people who broke their self-imposed silence and spoke to me. In addition, a few people spoke to me "off the record." Each of these conversations were powerful and gut-wrenching. I appreciate their willingness, patience and courage to share their memories. A list of the people who agreed to be interviewed follows.

I particularly want to thank Chief Robert Temple and Arnold Holbrook. Their unvarnished, firsthand accounts unlocked the box of understanding and answered so many questions that many of us harbored all these years.

I am also indebted to Larry Schieber and his sister, Karen Schieber Donnelly, who shared their memories, documents, photos, time, and an abundance of encouragement to write this story.

I tried my best to verify stories and rumors. Many details have been lost with the death of key people. I also sidestepped stories of personal misery and misfortune of people still alive who didn't want their heartaches told in public. I respected those wishes as best I could without compromising the facts surrounding this event.

I am grateful to the people in my life who supported me while writing this book. My husband, James Shuler, provided me with unconditional love and kindness when the stories overwhelmed me, and he gave me tutorials on the effects and management of trauma from his professional experience. My Foster brothers and sister gave me encouragement each step of the way for the past year, even while it was painful and sad to remember. And, in the end, sharing our stories has brought us closer together.

Special thank-you to my readers and editors: my sister, Karen Foster Nolan, Karen Schieber Donnelly, Gloria Alvarez, and Dr. Tru (Shayne) Leverette. Their job was made more difficult by the fact that this story was also their story in all the emotion and love for the characters in it.

And lastly, I thank my dad and my mom, who both did a great job providing good examples of how to live life with integrity and love.

"May the Lord bless you and keep you…"

Interviews

Brown, Dennis. Interviewed by Joni Foster. Phone call/recorded. July 9, 2016. (First on the scene.) Dennis spent most of his life as a missionary in different communities around the world. He retired a while ago and resides in Ohio, with his wife, in a suburb of Columbus.

Brown, Mike. Interviewed by Joni Foster. Phone call/recorded. July 21, 2016. (Former Fire Chief, Circleville.)

Donnelly, Karen Schieber. Interviewed by Joni Foster. Phone. August 21, 2016, and again December 2, 2016 in person. (Daughter of Charles Schieber.) Karen is married, living and working in Cincinnati. She has three children.

Foster-Nolan, Karen. Interviewed by Joni Foster. In person and phone. Various dates. Karen has spent the majority of her career in journalism and has lived for the past thirty-eight years in California. She is married and has two children.

Foster, Ty. Interviewed by Joni Foster. In person and phone. Various. Ty is an attorney, and lives with his wife in Cincinnati.

Grant, Teresa. Interviewed by Joni Foster. Phone. November 2016. (Granddaughter of Martha Lagore.) Teresa grew up in Mississippi, where she currently resides.

Gullick, Dean. Conversation with Joni Foster. In person. July 26, 2016. (Family friend.) Dean and his wife, Gloria Alvarez, also from Circleville, live in Houston.

Holbrook, Arnold and Edith. Interviewed by Joni Foster. In person/recorded. July 1, 2016, and November 22, 2016. (Son of Lee Holbrook.) Arnold and Edith live in Circleville.

Holbrook, Edith. Interviewed by Joni Foster. Phone. July 26, 2016.

Lindsay, Scott. Interviewed by Joni Foster. Phone call/recorded. July 18, 2016. (Stock boy at Bingman's Drug Store.) Scott retired from a long career in pharmacy, having worked in hospitals and corporate settings in the South. He currently lives in Georgia.

Mader, Jack. Conversation with Joni Foster. In person. November 2016. (Son of funeral home director.)

MacCahan, Tammy Sabine. Interviewed by Joni Foster. Phone. December 1, 2016. (Niece of Martha Lagore.)

Osborn, Karen. Interviewed by Joni Foster. Phone. August 16, 2016. (Family friend.)

Osborn, Janet. Interviewed by Joni Foster. Phone. August, 2016. (Family friend.)

Palm, Earl and Jeannie. Interviewed by Joni Foster. In person. May 25, 2016. (Family friend.)

Temple, Robert. Interviewed by Joni Foster. In person. May 2016 (with Larry Schieber) and November 29, 2016. (Former Circleville Police Chief.)

Tomlinson, Joe. Interviewed by Joni Foster. Phone call/recorded. July 18, 2016. (Stock boy at Bingman's Drug Store.) Joe married his high school sweetheart, Cathy Frericks Tomlinson, also from Circleville. Joe works in real estate and lives with his family in Greensboro, North Carolina.

Schieber, Larry. Interviewed by Joni Foster. In person. May 30, 2016. (Son of Charles Schieber.) Various follow up e-mails and calls. Larry and his wife, Kim, also from Circleville, have a pharmacy in Circleville, where they live and raised their two sons.

Willison, Charles (Chuck). Interviewed by Joni Foster. In person/recorded. November 21, 2016. (Husband of Francis Willison.) Chuck continues to live in the same house he did at the time of the event, about five miles outside of Circleville.

Willison, Jim. Interviewed by Joni Foster. Phone call/recorded. January 23, 2017. (Son of Francis Willison.) Jim lives with his wife in Indiana and has two adult children. After a long career in communications engineering, he presently does voice work for videos and commercials.

Endnotes

[1] Brian Doyle, "Everyone Thinks That Awful Comes By Itself, But It Doesn't," The Sun, No. 494 (February 2017): 21.

[2] Numbers 6:24-26 King James Version. The verse is: "The LORD bless thee, and keep thee; The LORD make his face shine upon thee, and be gracious unto thee; The LORD lift up his countenance upon thee, and give thee peace."

[3] "Hillbilly Highway," October 16, 2016. https://en.wikipedia.org/wiki/Hillbilly_Highway.

[4] Betty Dawley, "Top Local News Stories of 1967 Are Reviewed," Circleville Herald. December 30, 1967.

[5] "Weidemaier-Schieber Vows Read in Methodist Church," Circleville Herald, September 17, 1956.

[6] "Mass Funeral Rites Slated," Circleville Herald, April 17, 1967.

[7] "Damage in Area," Circleville Herald, February 16, 1967.

[8] Purchase contract provided by Larry Schieber.

[9] "Bingman Staff Proud of Remodeled Store," The Circleville Herald, Feb 2, 1967.

[10] "Happy New Year" advertisement, Circleville Herald, December 30, 1966.

[11] "Scranton Passes Exam as Pharmacist," Circleville Herald, March 25, 1964.

[12] "A Happy New Year Everyone!" advertisement, Circleville Herald, December 31, 1964.

[13] "Court News: Divorces Filed," Circleville Herald, March 15, 1967.

[14] "Mainly About People," Circleville Herald, September 22, 1954.

[15] "Lee V. Holbrook Files Complaint for Divorce," Circleville Herald, October 9, 1947.

[16] "Six Month Jail Term Decreed For Swalbaugh," Circleville Herald, October 15, 1947.

[17] Michael Gibson, "To Some People It Seemed World Had Come to an End," Circleville Herald, April 17, 1967.

[18] James Richards, "Despondent Husband Believed Responsible," Columbus Dispatch, April 16,1967.

[19] The Herald Staff, "Blast, Inferno Claim Lives of Five Persons," Circleville Herald, April 17, 1967.

[20] "Beyond Vietnam", Martin Luther King. April 4, 1967. New York, New York. http://kingencyclopedia.stanford.edu/encyclopedia/documentsentry/doc_beyond_vietnam/index.html

[21] "Richards' Return Is Awaited Here". Circleville Herald, April 14, 1967.

[22] "Dance" advertisement, Circleville Herald, April 14, 1967.

[23] Harold Snook, "Tragedy in Roundtown," June 1967. Harold's three-page essay, while never published, was found in the memory boxes of both Larry Schieber and Karen Foster Nolan. Harold's wife and daughter were on the sidewalk in front of J.C. Penney's at the time of the blast.

[24] Don Mathews, "Investigators Probe Circleville Explosion," Columbus Dispatch, April 17, 1967.

[25] Michael Gibson, "To Some People It Seemed World Had Come to an End."

[26] Howard Snook, "Tragedy in Roundtown."

[27] "Emergency List at Hospital Swelled by Explosion, Fire," Circleville Herald, April 17, 1967.

[28] "Blast Aftermath," Circleville Herald, April 17, 1967.

[29] James Richards, "Despondent Husband Believed Responsible."

[30] "Blast Aftermath;" and Mrs. Elizabeth Jones, "Much Help Made Available When It Was Vitally Needed," Circleville Herald, April 17, 1967.

[31] "A Portrait of Disaster," The Columbus Dispatch, April 16, 1967.

[32] "Blast Aftermath."

[33] "Investigators Probe Circleville Explosion", Columbus Dispatch, April 17, 1967.

[34] "Mayor Offers Thanks for Gallant Effort". Circleville Herald, April 17, 1967.

[35] "Blast Aftermath."

[36] "Blast Aftermath."

[37] In 1968, the Methodist Church merged with United Brethren Church to become the United Methodist Church. A United Brethren Church was located two doors down from the Methodist Church in Circleville. Both churches got new names, but the local congregations never merged.

[38] Matthew 11: 28-30 King James Version.

[39] "A Portrait of Disaster" The Columbus Dispatch, April 16, 1967.

[40] "In Retrospect" Circleville Herald, April 18, 1967.

[41] "A Portrait of Disaster."

[42] "Explosion Rips City; Seven Missing. Bomb Placed in Drug Firm Said Cause". Circleville Herald, April 15, 1967 (2nd edition)

[43] "Roundtown", Circleville Herald, April 20, 1967.

[44] Mrs. Marion Sines, "Sad Event of Saturday Will Long Be Remembered," Circleville Herald, April 19, 1967.

[45] Carolyn Focht, "Quiet Saturday Routine Jarred By Blast, Fire," The Columbus Dispatch, April 16, 1967,

[46] Carolyn Focht, "Quiet Saturday Routine Jarred By Blast, Fire."

[47] "Emergency List at Hospital Swelled by Explosion, Fire."

[48] The Herald Staff, "Blast, Inferno Claim Lives of Five Persons."

[49] Don Mathews, "Investigators Probe Circleville Explosion."

[50] "Body Identified as Bomb Carrier By Archeologist," Columbus Dispatch, April 18, 1967. Dr. Raymond Baby was the curator of archeology at the Ohio Historical Society and noted anthropologist at The Ohio State University.

[51] Mrs. Marion Sines, "Sad Event of Saturday Will Long Be Remembered."

[52] "In Retrospect," Circleville Herald, April 19, 1967.

[53] "In Retrospect."

[54] "Mass Funeral Rites Slated," Circleville Herald, April 17, 1967.

[55] "In Memoriam," Circleville Herald, Apr 15, 1970, 18.

[56] 2 Samuel 11 King James Version. 2 Samuel 12 goes on to show that God punished David for this "sin against the Lord", yet David continued, to become a great king.

[57] "Blast Aftermath."

[58] Howard Snook, "Tragedy in Roundtown."

[59] Mike Lorz, "Circleville Learns to Live with Biggest Tragedy," Citizen-Journal, April 17, 1967.

[60] "Police Continue Explosion Probe," Circleville Herald. April 26, 1967.

[61] Blake, "Ever Happen to You?" Circleville Herald, March 3, 1962.

[62] Steve Jones, "Double Homicide Shocks Village," Circleville Herald, December 24, 1964; and "Pickaway Farmhand Admits Killing Mate, Mother of 6," Circleville Herald, September 8, 1959.

[63] National Coalition Against Domestic Violence, www.NCADV.org/learn-more/statistics

[64] "Is American Woman Losing Femininity?" "Pheris Krieger Named Cubmaster," and "Blown to Bits by Home-Made Bomb," Circleville Herald, September 19, 1959, 5. (Italics added)

[65] Numbers 14:18; Deuteronomy 5:9 English Standard Version.

[66] Scott started at Ohio Northern but later transferred to and graduated from the Ohio State University, School of Pharmacy.

[67] This detail, the size of the box, conflicts with other accounts, but it is Chuck Willison's memory.

[68] Post-Traumatic Stress Disorder (PTSD)

[69] "Lagore Almost Cracks Magic Circle of 300," The Circleville Herald, January 25, 1962, 2.

[70] The F word stands for feminist, a very misunderstood word that even today can be used as an insult.

Made in the USA
Columbia, SC
19 September 2017